GOLF ADDICT
GOES EAST.

Also by George Houghton:

Golf Addicts Omnibus
Golf Addict Among the Irish
The Secret Diary of a Golf Addict's Caddie
Golfers Treasury
Golf Addict Strikes Again!
Addict in Bunkerland
I am a Golf Widow
Portrait of a Golf Addict
Golf Addicts on Parade
An Addict's Guide to British Golf
Golf on my Pillow
The Truth About Golf Addicts
Golf Addicts Through the Ages
Golf Addict Visits the U.S.A.
Full Confessions of a Golf Addict
More Confessions of a Golf Addict
Confessions of a Golf Addict
Calendar for Golf Addicts (annually)

GOLF ADDICT
GOES EAST

WRITTEN AND
ILLUSTRATED BY

LONDON
COUNTRY LIFE LIMITED

First published in 1967
by Country Life Limited
Tower House, Southampton Street, London, WC2
Printed in England by
Lowe & Brydone (Printers) Ltd London

© George Houghton 1967

Contents

CHAPTER ONE

Away We Go ... in a Purring Jet

WHEN THE GOLF WIDOW and I hurl ourselves into foreign golf trips, early planning usually runs amok. This time, the paper-travel chaos was very grim, until the efficient Miss Bisson rescued us at B.O.A.C. headquarters. With extraordinary speed she equated our golfing requirements with air routes and scheduled flights. An itinerary was prepared, and we were away.

The tour actually germinated in a letter from my nomadic golf buddy, Graeme Nicholl. Writing from Hong Kong, he said: 'I have taken on the Secretary's job at Shek O. Why not come out for a knock? The course will flatter your game'.

Disregarding the snide comment, I examined the photographs which accompanied Graeme's note. There was a colour picture taken from the air, showing 18 holes, a swimming pool, the lovely coastline, waving palms ... Also, there was a snap of a little cutie, captioned 'Kitty Wong—one of my assistants'.

Fair enough. This invitation to visit golf's ultimate could not lightly be tossed aside. I said so to the Golf Widow.

'A heck of a long way to go for a game of golf,' she muttered.

So we became involved in an outing which embraced Hong Kong, India, Thailand, Japan, Philippines, Singapore, Malaysia .. In fact, every darned place, it seemed, where golf addicts in southeast Asia indulge their splendid way of life.

The day before we emplaned from London airport, Tommy Docherty, the Chelsea football club manager, packed off his team to Bournemouth for golf, in preparation for a cup tie. Also, the third air disaster took place in Japan, bringing the total to 321 dead in a month.

These items occupied the headlines in newspapers handed to the Golf Widow by our air hostess. Taking comfort from the theory that golf is good for everything, and that a series of three air-craft misfortunes having already happened, a fourth was most unlikely, we settled down for the first stage of what could only turn out to be a lively marathon.

Measured and scaled up on the map, I totalled 24,600 flying miles. This would not take into consideration the dodging about we expected to do in big countries like Thailand, Japan and Malaysia but it would take in for my consideration more than thirty-three golf courses.

These days, it is all so easy—getting there I mean—and friendly. It took us two hours of cursing at lorry drivers before we reached London airport by car from our home on England's south coast. Then, in about the same length of time a great purring aircraft had skimmed us over the Alps and displayed lovely Florence, lying in the Italian sun beneath our starboard wing.

Without hesitation night descended, and on the intercom Captain Hart informed us that the island of Corfu was below, and I suppose before he had finished speaking we were nearly a hundred miles past. Later, he chatted informally with each of the hundred and seventeen passengers. As intended, this made us glow with confidence. Aeroplanes these days are really extensions of your own drawing rooms.

Although I am thoroughly familiar with the patter of golf, have a modicum of striking ability, and unbounded optimism in the future of my game, I know rock bottom zero about aircraft. But a commander does not invite one to join him on his flight deck every day of the week, so we went.

I have a set phrase which usually does when I get involved in discussions on mechanical things. I say, 'No doubt about it, the so-and-so is a nice little job'. Everything with wheels, engines, and gadgets is a 'little job'.

Without taking his eyes from the knobs, discs and thingummies, Captain Hart spoke slowly and what he said reduced me to the size of a low tee.

'This is the finest aircraft that our company has ever had in service,' he said, adding: 'There is no passenger aeroplane in the world like the VC.10'.

I asked him if he played golf. He didn't and that was really the end of our conversation.

Invariably, the crews of aircraft are very nice, hand-picked

We became involved in an outing . . .

people. Mr Tewkesbury, of Tewkesbury in Gloucestershire, was the chief of our corps of six stewards. He can bring babies into the world in full flight (he is a state registered nurse), and has many other accomplishments. In the watches of the night, we talked about the Anzio beachhead and the tobacco factory where I was cowering from German shelling while he was out fighting tanks and being taken prisoner.

'Tewk' introduced me to his lovely Miss Rafat Kazi, the daughter of a prominent barrister. Miss Kazi wears a uniform sari of bronze shot silk in winter, and pale blue gossamer cotton with toffee-coloured edging in summer. There are fifty Indian ladies among the B.O.A.C. air hostesses. I am sure they are all charming.

'Do you play golf?' I asked.

'No, but I love flying.' She said this with a pale-hands-I-love-beside-the-Shalimar look, and handed me a goblet of champagne to celebrate our crossing of the Holy Land.

That evening the Golf Widow and I dined on Canapé Lucullus, Devon Spring Chicken with devilled sauce, sliced beans panachée and marquise potatoes, then a shot of cordon bleu brandy to cut off the fermentation . . . And we were gliding down on Kuwait.

This patch of arid desert is no bigger than eight or nine eighteen-hole courses. Every native, if he wants to, can be richly pensioned at thirty, and the oil sheiks could buy koh-i-noors every day of the week. To land there at the midnight hour, with orderly lines of flame jets burning into the night just for the hell of it like ornamental fountains, is dramatic, and vaguely unsettling.

There was a little man selling things in the corner of the airport lounge. He had fine gold Swiss watches at trifling cost, French perfumes, and the well-known British and American cigarettes at 12s. 6d. for cartons of 200 cigarettes. Seated at a table, sipping Coca-Cola, was a posse of Sheiks in charcoal gowns with white burnouses. Slightly furtive, I thought, or perhaps merely shy. They did not appear to be travellers. Perhaps they just came to the airport for a glimpse of the western weirdies who emerge from air liners.

I asked a man who spoke a little English if the Kuwaiti had got down to the golf game. He said government officials and oil technicians played up country; then he said no he thought it was another game.

It took us three-and-a-half hours to reach Bombay. We didn't sleep, which was worth it to see the city from the air while approaching from the western sea. The lights were star dust, scattered carelessly but tight and orderly along the coast.

By the clocks, we were shedding hours and when we put down it was 6.20 a.m., local time. Bang on Miss Bisson's schedule and, let's face it, more punctual than most British trains.

In this part of India, night joins day with a pearly dawn lasting not more than ten minutes.

We completed formalities at Bombay's Santa Cruz airport. These included registering as 'an alcoholic drink imbiber', and being given a permit to function as such in India. Then the dawn was over and we burst out into the strong sunshine to be greeted by Sushi and Sirdari, our Indian friends, who quickly scooped us into their home product 'Ambassador' motor car.

Thoroughfares from towns to airports are nearly always crummy circuitous routes that ferret out the most dismal districts of any city. The highway into Bombay is no exception and if I call it Lavender Row, the name given by a friend, you will know what I have in mind.

Jack Hordern, six handicap, 'Mr Fixit' as he is called among West India's happy hackers, awaited us in his apartment on Malabar Hill.

There were two important things. First, Jack gave us a good breakfast. Then, he sprang a surprise. A terrific four-ball was scheduled to start a brief spell hence, and he urged us to hurry because we were all dashing off to Chembur, which is the Presidency Golf Club, twenty miles away.

Things couldn't have panned out better, said Jack. No business that day; all offices closed because the city was celebrating Holi day, an important fertility festival, like the old Roman Dionysus beano. On the way from the airport we had seen young people smeared with bright colours, mostly red. The idea is to squirt coloured water on those whom the squirter considers need fertilising. In this rather messy way a jolly time was being had by all, including some foreign visitors imprudent enough to open the windows of their motor cars!

Well, what with the fertility fracas (in a temperature of 90°), following a dozen sleepless hours in the purring jet, Jack's announcement that I was to perform in a distinguished four-ball brought home forcibly enough the fact that preliminaries were over. Now it was up lads and hit 'em.

Gently I was led to the bathroom for a resuscitating cold shower.

'You must be mad,' said my wife.

She'd said it often before. This time she was probably right.

CHAPTER TWO

Happy Bombay Breed

ON RARE OCCASIONS the Commanders of aircraft apologise for what they call 'slight turbulence'. In the stratosphere, turbulence means rough and I may say that on the Chembur course I saw plenty of turbulence. Under the circumstances, it was perhaps to be expected that my game should stray from the straight and narrow. Apart from putts.which rolled yards past the hole on the fast greens, I don't suppose I hit a single shot off the meat during the long hot day.

With my brand of golf, anything unusual conspires against good striking, and I think at this early stage I should mention a difficulty that is probably common to all of those in the golf writing trade.

I have written twenty books about the game, so not unnaturally perhaps, people expect me to perform rather well. For this reason, when playing with strangers during these golfing peregrinations, I am more anxious than usual to hit a good 'un from the first tee. This anxiety doesn't help and I usually produce a failure.

As a visitor, I am invariably offered the honour. Without too much fuss, I warn my host not to expect more than a fairly workmanlike job.

'My handicap is twelve at St Andrews,' I say, and add: 'But that was on score-cards taken out years ago.' Then I drivel on about getting old, and being slightly off-balance with travelling . ..

These preliminaries do not always prepare my new friends for what is to come. They always think I'm being modest—until we've played a few holes.

Now, although my game can be roughly categorised as that of a well-tutored dub, I doubt whether anyone gets more fun from golf than I do, and you can't have it all ways. As a matter of fact, leaving aside Joe Carr, who is phenomenal, I have yet to meet a

13

top-line golfer who can suck as much from the game as I can. You may ask how do I know? Well, of course, I can't be sure, but regularly I see tigers make for the club billiard room while I am splashing out to hack around in the rain. I honestly believe that all golf is good, although sometimes it is better.

Enough of me. But while on the subject of a golfer's performance immediately after travel, particularly air travel, I must toss in some relevant comments.

During this lengthy trip, taking off quickly from one golf centre to another like a hungry grasshopper, I noticed that my game deteriorated in direct ratio to the speed at which we covered the territory. If we were in a place for only one day my game was just twice as bad as it was when we remained for two days, and so on.

'Dindo' Gonzalez, about whom you are going to read later, has studied this aspect of golf. He cites the example of Gene Littler, who arrived by air from California and within an hour of arrival in the Philippines was playing red-hot competitive golf. At Wack Wack on the first day Littler shot a 77, second day a 76, third day a 70, and on the fourth round he scored a magnificent 68.

The other big thing in the Philippines is cock-fighting. 'If an owner lets his cock fight before resting for a couple of days after a journey, he can count on a dead bird,' says Dindo.

He has gone into the whole question meticulously, and he even produced for my benefit a well-known Manila doctor to expound on how travel, particularly in aircraft, upsets the equilibrium. The liquid in the middle-ear, or something . . .

Anyway, there you are, and I promise not to make any further excuses for my performances, on this trip at any rate.

The fairways at Chembur were very thirsty, and looked like the surface of a closely cut cornfield. Drought was in full season, and use of the limited water was carefully controlled. Rainfall in these parts never seems just right. It either comes down in buckets (Jack Hordern said he had known eleven inches in one night!), or you don't see a drop in months. At monsoon time Chembur has nine holes constantly under water, and in the dry season the ground is sometimes so hard that the caddie perches your ball up on a deftly folded piece of cigarette packet, because it is impossible to hammer a tee into the ground.

Nevertheless, here is a golf course with many attractions. There are some extraordinarily well-designed holes and although par is 71 and the extended yardage is only 6,200, no-one can take liberties with this track. The land is flattish, with trees, some undulations, and many natural hazards. Look over the 14th tee with the blue hills behind and white villas among palms and you are reminded of Valescure, on the French Riviera. Ice boxes are placed at strategic points on the course from whence drinks mysteriously appear; another novel feature, not quite so welcome perhaps but very useful to swell club funds, are small cartoon advertisement boards. They are discreetly placed and not the eyesore one would imagine.

Constant hazards at Chembur are the ball-thieving crows. You have two caddies, a bag carrier, and an *age wallah*, who gallops up to your ball when it comes to rest and covers it with a piece of blue rag. The rags used to be red, but the crows got wise, so now they are blue and soon they may have to be yellow. There are also hawks at Chembur, but crows are the main pest, so a crow is incorporated into the club badge.

Never mind the crows. They didn't affect the lady in our four-ball; she played an impeccable round of level fours. Thelma Brown's handicap is 2; she is Chembur Lady Champion and has been since 1960; also she is Champion of West India, and in 1962 was champion of all India. Hubby Harry is an old-timer out here, Past Captain of Chembur, and goodness what else. Also, he is a purposeful low-handicap golfer, and that also applies to Jack Hordern, who the previous week had played with the King of Malaysia. So you see the company 1 was keeping.

It was a miss-a-meal day (because of the famine) but over a plate of potato crisps and large tumblers of *limbu pani*—fresh lime juice, water, sugar and ice—we enjoyed golf gossip.

Thelma Brown told of the Makableshwar Golf Club, two hundred miles away, where she started her golf and where non-paying visitors include panthers and monkeys. This club was once a great spot for British army golfers on leave, and that goes back a while for the holes at Makableshwar are all named after Boer War battles, like Spion Kop.

Talk of monkeys reminded someone of the Delhi Golf Club where the trespassers had the endearing habit of larking about on the 6th green, and, using the flag as a club, giving a very fair

imitation of how their human cousins played golf. An unappreci-
ative committee soon put a stop to that and had the flag-stick
entwined with barbed wire!

Chembur village is mainly mud huts and here you see the less
attractive aspects of India. During the 1965 fighting the village
was used as a re-settlement area and if you drove out of bounds
at the 9th you were 'in Pakistan'. Most of the caddies live in the
village. Spindly little chaps, they are cheery as crickets, and have
a rare sense of humour. They start as *age wallahs* (saving precious
golf balls from the crows) at 1s. 6d. a round, then, as they get
to know about golf, they graduate to grade 1 caddies and earn
3s. 6d. a round. Many of the boys play good golf and I noticed
on the board in the lounge that the caddies nearly always win the
annual Caddies v. Members match.

A golfer who had once missed a short putt at Chembur did
the club-throwing act. His putter whizzed into a coconut palm,
brought down a nut which hit a caddie on the head. Quite
rightly, the lad ran off with the club and neither were seen again.

My caddie that afternoon was named Kishan. He was a man of
uncertain age who warmed my heart because he clapped hands
whenever I made a good shot. 'Licky' is the Chembur professional. He was also a little uncertain about his age, although
in no doubt whatever how to strike a ball nearly 300 yards.

There had been a double celebration at the club. A new 24-
handicap member named Mr Bose had holed in one. He was the
commander of an Air India aircraft, and that same day had arrived
from London, flying non-stop to Bombay via Moscow, where he
had been refused permission to land.

How high-spirited are the Bombay golfers, even on *limbu pani*!
The annual 'international' golf meeting is really something. When
we were there addicts were sparring around, hotting up the ex-
citement. Scotland, England, India, Japan, Scandinavia, Australia
and Canada (combined team) and the U.S.A. all compete in a
knock-out tournament. As can be expected it is sometimes rather
difficult to make up teams, but fortunately the nationality qualifi-
cation is loose. An Englishman was to play for the U.S.A. and
when asked why, he answered 'Our firm's got a branch there'.
A wild man named Sandy Oag was the Skipper of the Scottish
side. He had arranged for a Gurkha piper to bring in his team,
and sent a despatch to each of his men urging them (in the words

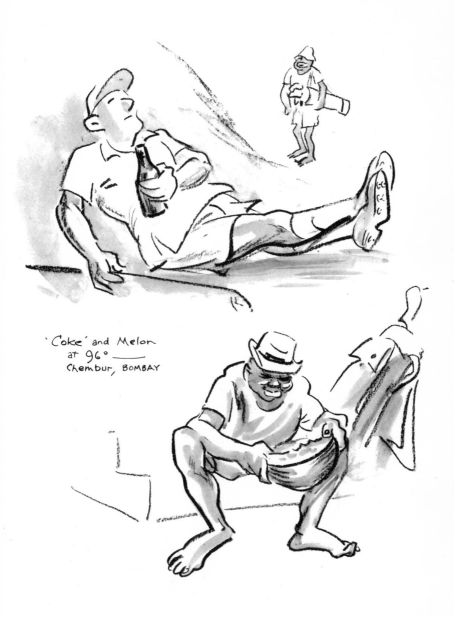

'Coke' and Melon
at 96° ———
Chembur, BOMBAY

At Chembur, drought was in full season

of Rob Roy) to 'go out and get the plunder'. Wild golf was in the air and it was a pity we would not be there to taste it.

As was proper, I paid my respects to the Captain of the Presidency Club, and from him I was overjoyed to learn, for the first time I am ashamed to say, of the Addicts Golfing Society of South India. This lively institution has a nominal role of more than six hundred members, sprinkled all over the world. The Society began in Madras in 1952, and annual golf meetings are held in the United States and in Britain. The motto is 'Easy does it', and the tie has a leaning-palm motif for a reason which is obscure.

As self-styled 'Golf Addict No 1', the least I could do was to offer a trophy, and this I am glad to say has been accepted.

Soon you will learn of many outrageously high golfing costs so I put on record that the membership subscription at the Bombay Presidency Golf Club was the lowest of any major club we visited. You pay 25 rupees a month, which is about equivalent to £30 a year. Cheap for what you get; this includes much good cheer and the regular sight of that beautiful golfer, R. K. Pitamber.

Rajkamur Pitamber, Prince of Nepal, or 'Pit' as he is widely known among golfers in India, played for Oxford University in 1951, 1952, 1953 and 1954. He is still a great striker. Still? I should say that right now in the year 1966 at the age of thirty-five Pit is at his prime. The week before we arrived he broke the record for the Willingdon course by returning a 56—10 shots inside par!

The Willingdon Sports Club, four miles from the city centre, still sniffs a little of Rudyard Kipling who, in fact, was born as near as a brassie shot with a following wind.

The original badge of the Willingdon Club incorporated the letters W.C., so for obvious reasons they brought in the word 'Sports'. Lush lawns, box hedges and old English flowers like London Pride are in the beautiful gardens, and indoors you find the quiet unobtrusive luxury of good timber, leather chairs, old portraits, and talk in discreet undertones.

Lord Willingdon was a Governor of Bombay and subsequently became Viceroy of India. He formed the Club in 1917 mainly for the pursuit of polo and cricket. There is a fine racecourse across the road, but at the Club the emphasis is now on golf. In the

The 5th.
at Willingdon
Bombay

old days, members were top government officials, admirals, generals and a few selected maharajahs. Then, the 'box wallahs' (business men) were accepted, but always with great discrimination. And that is the impression the visitor gets even now, in a vastly more democratic Bombay.

We chose a special occasion for our visit to Willingdon and this was partly to please the Golf Widow who wanted to see Ladies' Trophy Day, with *some competitors playing in saris*. Admittedly this is not customary, but at Willingdon it seemed right. As someone in our party said, golf in saris nicely links the mystic east with banks and braes o' bonny Doon.

Lady Kania, the widow of a former High Court Judge, knows all about Bonnie Doon, having played golf pretty thoroughly in Scotland. She is charming, and proud to be called an 'all weather' golfer. Lady Kania holds the unique distinction of having driven off the terrifying first tee at St Andrews in 1935, wearing a sari— and a handicap of 24! Always in a sari, this very brave lady has played famous courses from Sunningdale to Royal Sydney, Australia. She is a past captain of Willingdon Ladies, an honour which doubtless will one day go to her golfing daughter, Rukmini.

The ladies of Willingdon entertained us to some grand golf and honours went to a new friend, Anne Reeves, whose Stableford score of 47 points prompted her to say 'That settles it. I'm going to Wentworth to play in the Daks.'

Wentworth and Willingdon are centuries apart.

The course here is short, flat, but unusually beautiful. Flowering trees are everywhere, and Skipper Sultanali Micklai, who, as a boy, used to play with the elderly Aga Khan, told us of the different species. Even in drought, the greens are lush and weedless, despite the terrific traffic on what could well be the busiest golf course in India.

Once in a while, we get a fragment of news that restores hope that civilisation may survive after all. We picked up one such morsel from the Skipper of Willingdon who told us that he and his brother, whose home is in Pakistan, proposed to arrange an India *v.* Pakistan golf match. Naturally, I don't know what the state of affairs will be between these countries when this book reaches print, but at the time of the proposal it seemed wonderfully enterprising and furnished just one more instance when golf and goodwill can be employed more sensibly than guns and grumbles.

On departure, Skipper Mecklai told us he had been obliged to reprimand four of the senior Indian members.

'It was getting too bad', said the Skipper. 'This four-ball was holding up the whole course on three mornings every week. They started at 5.30 a.m. and when they reached the 6th green they used to settle down on the grass and eat a picnic breakfast, before playing the remaining three holes.'

A snack at 6.30 a.m. on the course did not seem so very irregular. Then we heard the details.

'It was taking longer and longer', said Mr Mecklai. 'The losers always paid and the meal was properly set out alongside the green which is near the clubhouse. On the day I complained, they had melon, waffles, kidneys on toast, steaks with fried eggs, toast, coffee . . . Even the caddies were having strawberry milk shakes!'

CHAPTER THREE

Contrasts — and a Pinch of Salt

THE WATERFRONT AT BOMBAY is a great handsome crescent, especially at night when the lights on Marine Drive have inspired the name 'Queen's Necklace'.

At one end there is Malabar Hill. We stayed there, quite close to the Parsee burial place where bodies are laid out on holy ground. At the other end of the crescent there is laid out and tended with loving care the United Services Golf Club.

Between the two points, mostly on land reclaimed from the sea, sprawls the great city of Bombay with more than 3,000,000 inhabitants.

Students walk six abreast in the roads, policemen conduct traffic in the shade of private sunshades fixed to their belts, women like goddesses in saris stroll elegantly about their shopping, huddled poverty sleeps in doorways . . . And right in the centre of the crescent, near Chowpatty Beach where political meetings are held, there are the sports clubs. These *gymkhanas* are separately assigned for Hindus, Parsees, Muslims and other sections of the community. Also there is the Bombay Club, which is only for Europeans and used to be the social centre for Britons in Bombay. Cricket, soccer, bridge, billiards and normal club activities flourish, but alas, there is no golf, nor has there been for many years. Nevertheless, and this is strange, in the Club's official handbook a golf section is still indicated (Mr J. Tate is the listed Hon. Sec.), although there has neither been a golf course nor even a meeting held for three decades. I suppose Mr Tate can claim to be the only unharassed secretary in the game—if he is in the game. It is all rather sad.

In the spring of each year the Royal and Ancient Golf Club of St Andrews play for the Bombay Medal and this was presented by the Golfing Society of Bombay (later to become the Royal Bombay Golf Club) in 1846.

Those were the great days.

I examined the early records and find that the club was formed in 1842 with a working committee, comprising the Captain, Treasurer, Secretary, Senior Counsellor, Junior Counsellor, Chaplain, Standard Bearer, and—wait for it!—Poet Laureate.

On special occasions, so the records say, the Skipper started his round preceded by the official standard bearer, and accompanied by Counsellors, his Chaplain, and a regiment of caddies. When things went well and the Captain sank a few long putts, no doubt the Poet Laureate got to work!

Despite high jinks in the early days, the long history of the Golf Society of Bombay makes sad reading. In 1847 it appears that the club declined and although there was a flicker of revival in 1855, it again slipped to near oblivion in 1861. But in 1869 a golfing Scot named Robert Stevenson got to work and he must have stirred things up because the Royal charter was given.

In 1875, the golf club was taken over by the Bombay Gymkhana and the first thing that happened under the new administration was that most of the course was turned over for building, which was inevitable, being in the very centre of a fast-growing city.

Nevertheless, right until 1938 golf was played on the stretch of land known as the Oval, which is really the green heart of Bombay, measuring about 1,000 yards by 200 yards.

The Golf Widow and I viewed the sward when about a quarter of a million Indians were strolling around in the cool of the evening. The Oval has always been public land, used for football, cricket and just strolling. As recently as 1938 the Royal Bombay Golf Club played there, but it must have been a golfing headache. Play started at dawn but had to finish by 9 a.m. to make room for the public. Bunkers were transportable canvas sheets and the positions were changed daily according to the caprice of the groundsman.

That is the dolorous tale of the Royal Bombay Golf Club. One day play somewhere may be revived. I hope Mr Tate hopes so.

Stepping from the cobwebs of the R.B.G.C. into the sparkle of the United Services Golf Club at the extreme southernly end of Bombay's Bay, was like plunging into a cool bath. Luckily for us, our visit coincided with the arrival of a breezy old sea salt (disrespect unintended) who had planned a spell of chipping practice in preparation for a blood match.

Rear Admiral S. G. Karmarkar, handicap 10, Royal Indian Navy, Rtd., almost made the United Services Golf Club with his own two hands. Major General Henderson-Brooke, an Englishman in the Indian Army, helped him. And also, of course, there were hundreds of coolies, plus what the Admiral called ancillary helpers. This simply meant that all soldiers and sailors confined to barracks at the Calaba base were put to work on the golf course!

Addicts will always find a way. First, the Admiral persuaded the authorities that the stretch of land by the sea should be made into a golf course for exercise and recreation. Then the job started. The site alongside a lovely beach was marvellous, but only scrub covered the area. There was no grass, or trees for shade; it was merely a flat stretch of dry barren land.

In due course, Admiral Karmarkar supplied all that was needed. He planted hundreds of *casuarina* trees; these are a species of wisteria and do very well. He solicited the help of Colonel Gurucharan, an officer who commanded a mule regiment—because the animals were useful on the course! During his service career the Colonel had been badly kicked, and although he got down to 7 handicap, the Admiral said 'he had the most remarkable swing, that started by going up in front instead of round to the right . . .'

So, in due course, golf at the Calaba base became a reality. When the course gasped for water the Admiral hinted to his medical officer (also a golfer) that the pool should be temporarily condemned for bathing, but usable on the golf course.

In 1962 the United Services Golf course was the best in Bombay. When we were there it was very sunbaked, but even now many members (non-service personnel admitted) join merely for the four wonderful weeks following the monsoons when everything is green and lovely, and you crack off at the water's edge and enjoy a swim after nine holes.

The clubhouse is an old officers' mess and there is a banyan tree in a patio, with chickens pecking around. Delightfully simple, picturesque in a South American way, and as different to the Willingdon as my brand of golf is to Arnold Palmer's.

The Admiral has now retired from the Navy and is very much

a businessman. He is, of course, also very much a golfer, and explained that he couldn't possibly stay in his office when it was being painted, an operation which I understand is necessary every few weeks!

We learned of a great golf match which took place between the Presidency Club and the United Services. Later, there was a banquet aboard the Admiral's aircraft carrier and every golfer was piped aboard, which is splendidly as it should be.

We left the Admiral busy at his chipping, and drove back to Malabar Hill for luncheon with our Indian friends Sushi and Sardari.

Pomfret is a delicious flat fish caught in the bay, and this was served as a prelude to tandoori spiced chicken roasted in a clay oven and served with dahl sauce made with six varieties of lentils . . .

We took off from Bombay's Santa Cruz airport at first light. When you fly at that ungodly hour, you really leave the day before, for there is the long ride down 'Lavender Row' and the usual departure formalities.

Preparation for our flight was an all-night party with Bombay's golfing fraternity. 'Pit', the Admiral., the Browns, and the twenty or so other addicts whom Jack Hordern had herded, were in terrific form . . . Then we were in the aircraft and the contrast was breathtaking.

In the normal way, even the sight of these great jets fills me with terror. They look so diabolically mechanical, and clinical. But at Indian dawn it wasn't like that. The giant wore a softening wrap of morning mist and the engine was at rest. After the good-bye jollifications, by contrast everything was quiet. At the head of the gangway, an Indian hostess welcomed us with the hands-in-prayer gesture, and 'Namasty', murmured with a kindly smile. Inside the aircraft, Puccini's 'One fine day' was playing softly, and we were handed iced towels, moistened in lavender water to smooth away the last of Bombay. Cool orange juice, a glance through *The Times of India*, and the purring started.

In less than two hours we landed at Dum-Dum airport, Calcutta.

Until 1896 there was a 9 holes golf course where the big jets now roar. In fact, the early India Championships used to comprise two rounds over Dum-Dum and one over each of the 9

holes Maidan courses. History must be limited for this entails long pauses for research and there was so much to see and so many courses to play. But Calcutta is special, being the oldest golf club in India. In fact, this is also the oldest golf club outside Britain; even in England only Royal Blackheath is as old as Royal Calcutta, although there are eleven clubs in Scotland with longer histories.

No-one can dispute the fact that Calcutta golf is not what it was. But the intriguing question remains: Where did the Calcutta golfers in the year 1829 previously play? In England there was only Royal Blackheath and it is unlikely that Calcutta's early hackers came from there. Much more likely that those who started the game on a stretch of flat land where the airport now stands came from Scotland where even in 1829 the game was popular. I had the bright idea that possibly officers of the Black Watch, or some other Scottish regiment stationed in Calcutta,

started the swinging. But I was wrong. Without any doubt whatsoever the little gang of addicts who got golf going in Calcutta came from Dundee and were engaged in the jute trade. Proof of this is furnished by the names of the early India Champions; they all came from Tayside.

Early records of the Royal Calcutta Club have been carefully preserved. Play started when George IV was monarch and the Iron Duke of Wellington was Tory Prime Minister. A Royal Charter was granted to the Club in 1912 by King George V, who (so 'tis said) once flicked a divot with his cane when walking on the course, which is as near as he ever got to playing golf.

Nowadays, membership is about 1,500, and this is probably the highest ever. The ancient rule excluding lady members has been rigorously upheld over the years and the arrangement whereby families can play seems to work. But sinister forces are at work . . .

As with the club known as Royal Bombay, the playing site of the Calcutta Club has changed many times. The course is now at Tollygunge, which resembles a lovely English park with un-English flowering trees, but the club motto is still 'Far and Sure', chosen it would seem by someone with a yearning.

The best golfers in India, quite rightly, live in the capital and play at the Delhi Golf Club. We wanted to see the man whose name echoed wherever we went, but he was absent.

Mr Ashok Malik comes of a golfing family and both I. S. and A. S. Malik are in the record books. Ashok was All India Champion in 1965. He won this with a score of 282, which was ten shots lower than Peter Thomson's score when he became Open Champion at New Delhi in 1963. And Peter doesn't play in a beard and turban!

We left India in an aircraft named 'Dhanlagari', one of the Himalayan peaks, and as I climbed aboard someone thrust into my pocket a copy of the South India Golf Addicts' song.

> *I'm a Member of the Addicts*
> *And golfing is my game,*
> *I cannot chip, I cannot putt,*
> *But I play it just the same.*
> *I play not for the glory,*
> *I play not for the cup,*
> *I play for what's inside it—*
> *I hope there'll be enough!*

Goodness knows what my neighbour thought as I hummed 'The Church's one foundation' en route for Thailand.

CHAPTER FOUR

Thailand with a Smile

A FRIEND OF MINE who is a senior British officer was entertained by a Thai general. This is the account I received in England, long before I planned to see for myself:

'The Thais are great ones for protocol, so the whole visit was a kaleidoscope of motorcades, bands playing European music without conviction, vins d'honneur, garlands, etc., but the high spot, and the most important thing in South-East Asia now, was the official game of golf.

'I don't know whether I've mentioned to you how the Asiatics have embraced this game, Establishment and intellectuals alike. My theory is that it's popular because you do not stand against your opponent and win or lose face to face with him, but oppose him as it were obliquely, so that being beaten does not seem so bad.

'Anyway, I was down to play with a general, and I was nervous because I am not really a golfer at all; I mean I have a set of clubs but I have no handicap.

'We each had two caddies, one carried the clubs and the other a stool and an umbrella in case we felt faint, which was likely enough with the temperature around 100°.

'The caddie with the bag handed my club to the caddie with the stool, who handed it to me, first polishing it.

'About a dozen men went on ahead to spot the fall of the shots, and three movie camera-men and half-a-dozen still cameramen burnt up miles of film as they followed us around.

'On every second tee a table was set up with a white cloth and iced drinks. All that was needed to complete the picture was a pair of swaying elephants, or a number of houris being carried behind in litters. This great assembly, like a tribal migration in a film by Robert Flaherty, poured slowly over the Royal Thai Air Force Golf Club at Don Muang, a few miles from the capital.

'What made it so rich was that in the centre of all the attention, the General and I were playing appalling, excruciating golf. His technique was to do a short war-dance before topping the ball eighty or ninety yards straight ahead; mine was to fire off great gusty shots into the jungle, where the distant crack of the ball striking a forest giant was echoed by a screech of parakeets and an angry chattering of monkeys.

'After three hours of hell, during which my face gradually became frozen in an idiot smile of diplomatic politeness, the General won by maintaining a standard one degree less contemptible than mine, and then all I had to do was to face up to the banquet (with speeches) in the evening'.

I deliberated a while before asking my friend for permission to reproduce his letter. One hates to cause offence. Then, I said to myself, damn it we're all in this golf game together and we expose our frailties and idiosyncrasies to whoever cares to peep over the golf course fence. The word Bangkok means 'City of Angels', and I hope the General (whom I met) will be one and laugh angelically, if not uproariously, when he reads what I have had to say.

To appreciate golf in Thailand you must first know the setting. To begin with, Bangkok, the capital, is a city where about 2,000,000 happy souls dwell in a place partly laid out like Hollywood, with wide straight boulevards and neon signs, advertising everything from American cars to Japanese fertilisers. Skyscrapers, hotels and even new temples shoot up overnight. But also there are the lovely houses in picturesque places, and canals and waterways which become floating markets every morning. There is the beautiful Emerald Buddha and three hundred other temples, royal barges, snake farms . . . And things you can find nowhere else in the world.

We came for golf and laughs. But you can't laugh when a man gets his jaw broken in the local boxing ring where kicks are allowed. Also there is cock fighting; kite-flying duels, with knives attached to the tails; log-moving elephants which each do the work of forty men . . . The famous 'white' elephant that is the symbol of Thailand has pink eyes and twenty toes instead of the normal eighteen.

At this point, to gain breath, here is a true elephant story which the Golf Widow read from the Bangkok English newspaper.

A lady had a little red motor car. She went into a shop and when she came out the bonnet of her car was squashed. Most apologetically a man explained that his elephant loved to sit on little red cars. With difficulty, the lady drove towards a garage. En route, she ran into a crowd gathered around a street accident. An ambulance drove up, and naturally the attendants thought the lady and her crushed car were involved. The lady protested and explained that an elephant had sat on her little red car. . . . She was taken away for shock treatment.

Because the street surfaces are too hot no-one ever walks in Bangkok, unless on stilts. The citizens buzz about in large shiny American cars, or in nippy little three-wheel taxis which are so cheap that even shop assistants and golf caddies use them to go to work.

But two things in Thailand stand out above all else. When folk speak they smile, and Thai ladies in their lovely *panung* dresses have the tightest, neatest little waists of any cuties in the world.

'Land of the free—Home of the Smiles' is thoroughly plugged in international travel offices by General Chalermchai, who is head of Thai tourism, but he gets into the book because of his position in the vanguard of golf fanatics.

Photographs of a plumpish backswing decorate the General's office, he plays at Royal Bangkok three times a week, and regularly finds it necessary to inspect the golf courses at Bangphra and Kowyai which are partly sponsored by the Tourist organisation. Also, he does Gary Player's press-up exercises.

In Thailand, golf is an accepted part of every army officer's training. With the Air Force, it applies even more, and the Royal Thai Air Force course at Don Muang, about fifteen miles from Bangkok, is about the best course in the country. The Open is usually played there. Politicians, it would seem, get their posts in the government according to golf handicap. Most pleasingly, the game has asserted itself in this happy country and, so far as we could see, everyone prospers.

The peaceful, gentle, strolling game we play in Europe and America, in Thailand is a part of life that is so important that any non-golfer who interrupts a 'crocodile' in full play runs a good chance of sudden death.

The 'crocodile' is a form of golf that must cause considerable anguish to local purists. Short of sending a gunboat and landing party, I fear there is nothing the R. and A. can do. The Thai Golf Association mildly disapproves, but the participants are such high-level citizens and so very obviously have a good time that maybe official crocodile tears will continue to fall.

'Crocodiles' are particularly popular at the Royal Dusit Club, where golfers sometimes tee off ten at a time. With caddies for bags, stools, umbrellas and beer, a caravan of as many as thirty folk sometimes sets off. Get behind a crocodile and it's death! Play is terrifyingly serious and why skulls are not cracked is a miracle. Golf balls fall from all directions, and meanwhile an accountant, who comes along with his notebook especially to do the complicated job, keeps careful tally of how many shots each player takes. This part is essential because many bets have been wagered; each player against 'the field' at every hole, team matches; nearest to the flag on short holes; longest drive, and so on. . . .

At the end of the match, which takes about four hours for 9 holes (a match is always 9 holes in Thailand, and it is not exceptional for addicts to play five 'matches' a day) the accountant goes into a corner to prepare a balance sheet. Meanwhile, those involved play poker dice for trifling bets of anything up to £20 a throw.

Let us not get things out of proportion. I have told you about the 'Crocodiles' because this is that kind of book. Nevertheless, serious golf is played here and some of the Thai players are outstandingly good. Without further ado I propose to list the eleven Thailand golf clubs which were in play when we were there. Others are under construction to help to cope with the astonishing demand.

In the first place, because it was established back in 1901, I list the Royal Bangkok Sports Club. The others are more or less in order as 'tests of golf'. These are Pat O'Connell's priorities. The Golf Widow and I couldn't visit them all, but as Pat is Deputy President of the Thailand Golf Association (the President is Thanat Khoman, the Foreign Minister), we will take his word.

Bangphra, where the caddies are all girls; Royal Hua Hin, by the sea, where the Thais really started the game, was laid out in 1909 by a Scot who was chief engineer on the Siamese railways; Royal Thai Air Force Club, at Don Muang; Royal Dusit; Cheingmai Gymkhana Club; Kowyai; Royal Thai Army course

Bangkok

In Thailand, golf is an accepted part of life

at Songkhla; Phuket; Lampang; and the Royal Thai Army course at Bongkhaen. There will be more before this list is in print for as someone said, new courses in Thailand are laid out and grow quicker than your beard.

Many golf centres are not yet 'clubs' in the accepted sense. Quite rightly, the course comes first, then the clubhouse and other amenities. As example, the new course at Kowyai could well become the best club in Thailand, according to Mr O'Connell. Accounts from other sources confirmed that opinion, although we did find in this fascinating country nothing differs so much as opinion.

Opinions don't matter if you have plenty of Thailand currency. We hadn't, so tried our luck in the 'Thieves Market', which is where you get the bargains in the Kasem district of Bangkok. The stall owner's opinion of a correct price will do, if you are rich. But if you are as impecunious as most, then your opinion of a fair price differs and you must haggle. And while on this subject, it is as well to remember that the Thais love a good haggle and will like you better if you so indulge.

Now, although haggling simply does not exist in the nice golf which addicts play, a certain amount of bargaining has been known to take place in the east.

Heard across a sunbaked fairway: 'All right, 7 then. But if I accept your 7 at the 9th, you must agree to my 6 at the 4th'.

Never mind. The Thais are keen and, as mentioned, they are the world's happiest people.

CHAPTER FIVE

Bangkok—and Englishmen
Go out in the Mid-day Sun

GOLF IS ON THE MARCH in Thailand. More courses are needed, particularly for youngsters with little cash. In the meantime there is not too much grumbling.

An American General, staying in our hotel while on leave from the Vietnam war, said: 'Bangkok is the laughingest city in the world. Smile with the Thais and you will be branded amigo.'

Folk laugh their heads off, but I am not sure whether we joined in, having soon realised that our visit coincided with the broiling season. The temperature fluttered around 100°, and when we stepped from the fully air-conditioned Erawan hotel it was like moving into the hot-air drying machine in a hairdresser's shop. Only it was damp.

To warm things up even more, the Thais flavour the food with a spice called *prikeenoo*. Get a grain in your mouth and you are a volcano! Even locals call prikeenoos 'small torpedoes'.

Still on background, but leading up to golf. The more recent Thai rulers are listed Rama IV (Yul Brynner in *The King and I*); Rama V, who started golf in Thailand; Rama VI, who, so far as I could judge, was a good and kindly ruler. Then came Rama VII, who was completely golf-addicted. This monarch eventually abdicated, but not before he had really lit the golf flame in his country.

The political regime in Thailand is now a constitutional monarchy, and all goes well with peaceful prosperity. At least, that was the impression when we were there. King Bhumibol Adulyadej is on the throne at the time of writing and although I regret to report that he is not a keen golfer, he sees to it that the pleasant 9 holes layout within the palace grounds is well-nursed for his guests.

It would not be an exaggeration to say that two-thirds of Thai Government officials and at least three-quarters of all service officers are golfers. Some of them were playing when I attacked the Royal Bangkok course. And this was most strange for the following reason.

I badly wanted to try out the terrain of which I had heard plenty and which was plainly visible from the verandah of our hotel apartment. Unfortunately, times for golf are booked long ahead and it took the wiles of Pat O'Connell to lay it on. He telephoned the professional, who said the only time available was at 1.15 p.m. on the following day. Only mad dogs and golf nuts would go out in the mid-day sun at Bangkok, and I am convinced that the time offered was the Professional's polite way of shooing me off. 'Okay,' I said, 'count me there.'

I expected that we would simmer alone. It seemed unlikely that local parishioners would scorch in the mid-day sun. But I was quite mistaken, for a cheerful man named Prince Chote beamed at us on arrival and announced he was just off for an hour on the practice ground before playing a match against Prince someone else.

Then I met Norman Anderson, an American who was involved in the kind of rare incident that can only occur at golf. Furious at missing a tiddler putt on the 2nd green at Royal Bangkok, he flung his club into the air. It struck a high-tension wire and fell to the ground, completely disintegrated. As if this wasn't enough for the story, it turned out that the putter wasn't his property, but had been borrowed from one of the four-ball who were following!

We met Colonel Varapon Israngkura, Thailand's Addict No 1, who learnt his golf while studying medicine in England and says he won't stop practising and worrying until he reduces his handicap by twelve shots. This, I was told, would just bring him into the single-figure bracket.

A huddle of very top-strata Thai lady golfers awaited their turn on the tee. I was told they would surely be the wives of cabinet ministers. Although some were snappily attired in the usual shorts, peak caps, and sockettes, one or two wore long sleeves, gossamer scarves, and parasols as protection from the sun, which was already—and we were partly under cover—reducing me to a moist rag. Yet, Mrs Pat Stewart, the Lady Champion, looked cool and lovely. . . .

**Top-strata Thai lady golfers . . . the wives of
cabinet ministers**

I mention these people as proof that I was not the only addict prepared to expose his golf to the heat of a Bangkok day.

Arrangements could not have been better. The Professional at Royal Bangkok was Glyn Jones; I say *was* because I suspect that by the time you read this he will have moved to pastures new. Like many of his ilk, Glyn has ants in his pants.

Because this type of pro is a 20th-century counterpart of the wandering minstrel, I propose to sketch in his nomadic career, before telling of our game in which we were joined by Jim Shaddy, old-time American trader and former flier in the U.S. Air Force.

Glyn Jones is the son of a Montgomeryshire schoolmaster. He played scratch golf at the age of seventeen, was amateur champion of mid-Wales, and played in the 1959 Carris side against a team of professionals. Jimmy Adams offered him an assistant's job at Royal Mid-Surrey, where he worked for two years. Then he went as assistant to Trevor Allen at Richmond. With David Mills he won the Sunningdale Foursomes. The lads got ambitious and having saved £100 each, fixed themselves with jobs at the Royal Calcutta Golf Club. While waiting, they went to Germany, gave lessons at Hamburg, Celle, Garmisch and Berchtesgarten. Then came a shock. The boat which was to have taken them from Genoa to India was full. Undismayed, the lads took the Orient Express, a dozen or two different motor coaches and other means of overland transportation, until, some weeks later, mostly riding rough, they reached Calcutta at the cost of only £40 each! They worked in Assam, Cawnpore, and goodness knows where else. David Mills then came home to England, and Glyn Jones signed as Professional at Royal Bangkok.

'What's the golf like in Beirut?' he asked. 'I've always fancied Lebanon. . . .'

I don't know whether Glyn will ever be a Jack Nicklaus, but my word he gets around.

Royal Bangkok is flat and somewhat involved with the race-course, although racing is never allowed to interfere with golf and small boys with green and red flags are employed to control the traffic. Criss-crossing the fairways, there are canals, called *klongs*; these provide rather unnatural hazards but add to the fun.

For our three-ball we had five caddies, three bag-carriers (in Grade A blue shirts) and two 'klong' boys, who were to swim in the coffee-coloured canals to retrieve mis-hit golf balls. These human tadpoles are lowly paid, I thought, and don't even get their three baht (about 1s 3d) if *they lose a ball*. Outside the Caddie Master's shop I noticed a 'Caddies' Complaint Box'; whether or not the boys could read the label is another matter.

My sherpa was a senior named Im, who proudly wore a green camouflaged linen hat from the Vietnam war. When he wanted to accelerate the speed of my putt he shouted 'taxi, taxi', and to indicate where my aim should be he would say 'Three balls top side', which is certainly better than talking in inches.

Most of these chaps are fine natural golfers and one of them named Dom Bruht did a 63 the day after Dai Rees took 70 in an exhibition match.

Jim Shaddy asked his caddie to pass him a bottle of beer from his golf bag. But the last bottle had gone.

'Trouble is,' grumbled. Jim, 'there are too many folk playing from one bag!'

Then he told me of the Thai policemen who live in a barracks overlooking the 4th green. They had trained a pet monkey to go down and steal golf balls. This was a great joke (for the bobbies) until someone put into effect the old monkey-capturing trick. The inside of a coconut was hollowed out and filled with rice. The thief put his hand in, grasped the rice, was too greedy to let go, couldn't get his hand out, and was easily caught.

Shaddy is a member of the Royal Bangkok Sports Club because, being a business man, it is essential. There are about a thousand foreigners in Thailand and of these, four hundred and fifty are British residents living in Bangkok. Some are in trade, but many are embassy officials. Nearly all use the Club where for a modest entry fee and about £2 a month there is golf (5,148 yards—par 67), horse-racing, cricket, soccer, rugger, tennis, badminton and a nice swimming pool, in addition to normal social and eating facilities. The Royal Bangkok Sports Club is situated bang in the centre of the city, so the value is unquestionably good for modest cash outlay.

Of the other golf clubs in Thailand, possibly the most popular is Hua Hin. Here is a glorious family links in a summer resort about 140 miles from Bangkok. Sample it on the special golfers' express train that operates each weekend; you will also be entitled to reduced hotel rates. We found it cooler here. Golf addicts are thoroughly pampered in Thailand, and that, of course, is as it should be.

Back to the Erawan (possibly the best hotel we experienced during the entire tour) where the Golf Widow wallowed in the pool, while I splashed through 18 holes of perspiration golf. So far as I could gather 'Erawan' means a three-headed, virile elephant. But I may be wrong, which I frequently was in Thailand because the pronunciations of certain letters of the alphabet are at complete variance to the sounds we know. The Thais pronounce L like N, S like T, and R like L. So when a voice on the Erawan loudspeaker system announced 'Nocan ttolmt' (which it seldom does!) the speaker could mean 'Local storms'. . . .

The most notable thing about golf in Thailand is that when you go there you want to do something else. This country really is the traveller's dreamland, and the Thai go to endless trouble to show you around.

Have a knock on the lovely links at Hua Hin. You may stay on for ever, and one day I might join you.

CHAPTER SIX

Chinese Crackers in Hong Kong

WITH A SOB in the pen, I must record that Hong Kong is worse off, golfwise, than it was thirty years ago. I mean for facilities. And this, in one of the fastest-growing, richest cities in the world is a burning shame which I hope and trust someone is doing something about.

I went into all this very thoroughly and these are the facts:

More than thirty years ago, when the population was three million less than it is to-day, there were nine golf courses, making 108 holes; to-day there are only five courses, adding up to 72 holes.

Four of the courses come under the auspices of the Royal Hong Kong Golf Club, which has 3,000 members and nearly 600 on the waiting list. Then there is the Shek O Country Club (18 holes) which is limited to only 300 members, all of whom must be 'westerners'; 75% British.

To-day, the population of the colony exceeds 4,000,000.

I must not elaborate this grim golfing situation because the Hong Kong space shortage is aggravating enough without Houghton's natter. But in 1934, in addition to the courses afore-mentioned, there was a British army course at Kowloon; a 9 holes course for resident Portuguese; Shatin G.C. for the Japanese; and Happy Valley, which alas, now has no happy hackers.

Hong Kong golf started at Happy Valley—a wide gorge cutting deep into the city—following an advertisement which the Hong Kong Club (an aged and greatly revered social institution) placed in local newspapers in 1889. People interested in golf were asked to attend a meeting. Only thirteen turned up, but these included two addicts whose names were Captain Rumsey, R.N., and

Gershom Stewart, who had been hitting golf balls up and down the race-track months before. Captain Rumsey was made Skipper of the new golf club and these duties he fitted in with his job as Harbour Master.

A good start. The club got under way, and a 9 holes course was 'drafted out' on the race-course—which was already accommodating polo, football and hockey. Somehow or other, golf got going. It was holeless (they had to aim at markers), and bunkerless, but it was nursed by fanatics who would probably have 'managed' if the only land available had been a volcano crater.

The first match was played in 1890 against the Argyll and Sutherland Highlanders. Membership of the club was then 100 and the clubhouse was described as 'a dark and cavernous place under the grandstand'. Nevertheless, there was pleasing decorum, and a minute was recorded by the Captain: 'The matter of members' dress has called for much adverse comment during the year . . . Your flannels either get yellow when they are washed, or when they are not they assume an even less desirable hue'.

The ladies had clamoured for their own pitch and by 1897 nine excellent holes were acquired at Deep Water Bay. In that year, Queen Victoria granted the Royal Charter, and the club was away. An excellent lunch was available, usually comprising 'cold saddle of mutton, cold gooseberry pie, and Watson's dry sherry—one dollar'. Good victuals for sixpence.

But the addicts wanted more. In those days, land was available at the right price, so an extended course was laid out in 1911 across the water at Fanling. Now, please note what a member was prepared to do for golf on a full length (though very rough) course. First, he crossed by boat to Kowloon, then he took a two-man rickshaw up a road of sorts for two or three miles as far as the Kowloon reservoir, then by foot to the police launch which crossed to a place called Taipo, from whence a smart pony ride took him to Fanling.

Those were the days.

The railway had started by 1916. The men golfed after their cricket on Saturday afternoons. They would dine and play poker until 2 a.m., arise at 7 a.m., play 18 holes, have a heavy steak breakfast, sleep until 4 p.m., play another round, dine and play poker until 1 a.m. sleep, breakfast, and back for duty on the 8.15 a.m. train.

At this stage in the history of Hong Kong golf, we'll pause for my pleasant four-ball game at Fanling with the Governor, His Excellency Sir David Trench; Commissioner of Police Henry Heath; and Graeme Nicholl, who had come over from Shek O for the occasion.

I could not have found more knowledgeable companions and I only hope they will forgive me for wrecking the game by bombarding them with questions.

The two 18-hole courses at Fanling have been laid out expertly on undulating land, among trees of many species. In places the rough resembles the angry stuff you get at Walton Heath, the fairways are good, and the terrain is more or less surrounded by handsome purple hills that someone quickly points out is China.

In fact, Fanling is very close to the frontier and on the motor-ride to the club Henry Heath diverted a mile or two to show us one of his observation posts overlooking what some people regard as the sinister land of China. It couldn't look more peaceful. Sentries sauntered, taking casual interest in the fishermen throwing their nets from sampans drifting down the Pearl river dividing the New Territories from China. They might well have been British troops behaving exactly the same. We clearly saw the Chinese villages of Kaktim and Shataukok, where the demarcation line actually passes down the middle of the main street.

The greens at Fanling are nearly always good. Most of the playing surface is covered with an adaptation of gezira and uganda grass which travelled as a shoe box full of seeded soil from Uganda to Cairo during the last war. This flourished in Egypt, then one single sod of the grass was flown from Cairo to Hong Kong in 1951 and from this small handful of turf there developed the splendid greens we know to-day.

The line-up for our match was 'H.E.' and Henry Heath versus Nicholl and Houghton and after the first three holes I could see that the result was a foregone conclusion. Details of the game will therefore be skipped, for which most will be thankful.

The first hole on the 'Old' course is marred by a road which was built right across the fairway by a non-golfing soldier for use during the Korean war. Henry Heath told how Chief Justice Clunie once hit a 'bus with his tee shot and the driver trotted across and returned the ball with a bow!

Behind the second green there is an ancient Chinese burial

ground. Parties come for picnics on memorial days.

Many of the fairways at Fanling are lined with forests and I had seen little groups of women crossing in single file and vanishing among the trees. They wore large straw hats heavily fringed with black and this is the characteristic dress of the Hakas, a nomadic 'guest' people who don't stay anywhere for long although they moved rather quickly when Nicholl shouted 'Fore!'

The scenery in the outward nine is particularly attractive. Houses with green-tiled roofs are tucked among the banyan and eucalyptus trees and sometimes you are even reminded of holes at Wentworth, an illusion which quickly vanishes when you are near enough to a house to hear the Chinese radio music.

By the 9th green there is a lovely English flower garden with geraniums, hollyhocks and marigolds. This was planted and cared for by Mr Frank Hunter, who, at the time of writing, is the Secretary at the Royal Lytham and St Anne's Golf Club, at St Anne's in Lancashire.

The 10th hole at Fanling is called 'Tommy Tucker' for an amusing reason. From the tee, the green is hidden behind a steep hill that rises almost perpendicular and must be carried if the player is to get his par four. The caddies climb the hill to see if the land is clear for the drives. If you know Chinese you shout to your fore-caddie 'Tak m tak ah? meaning 'Can I go?' Try it, and you will see why the hole has been named 'Tommy Tucker'.

Before tackling Tommy Tucker, most golfers linger at the Chinese shelter to suck in something cool and fruity. We did, and Sir David Trench entertained us with stories of golf in the Solomon Islands, where he had been Governor. At Honiara, which was built as an American Air Force fighter base, a 9 hole course was laid out and even twenty years after the main hazards are unexploded shells! The clubhouse is a shack. At one end a notice-board says 'Honiara Airport'; at the other end a board says 'Honiara Golf Club'.

We learnt of a sparkling incident which once took place at Fanling. In a high-level, four-ball match, one of the players did the first seven holes 3, 3, 3, 3, 3, 5, 3. This incredible scoring, four inside par, had the opponents' teeth gnashing. One of them was Kim Hall, a red-hot little Welsh international golfer.

'If this so-and-so gets another 3 I'm quitting,' said Kim.

Whereupon a twenty-five foot putt dropped for the seventh 3 in eight holes!

Fanling
HONG KONG

A road runs alongside the 8th fairway and at that precise moment a motor 'bus appeared. Taking Kim at his word, the other three bundled him aboard!

For the record, the four chaps involved in the lark were Alan Sutcliffe (who performed the super golf), Dick Carroll, John Mackie and of course Kim. All have been champions of the Colony and county golfers in England. It is appropriate to mention that Sutcliffe and Hall are prime movers in the organisation for the Far East Professional Golf Tournament. In fact, without Kim's early efforts the tour would not exist.

These notes about Hong Kong started with the regrettable item about shrinkage in golf facilities. But there is a ray of hope. Kim Hall showed me his plan to ease the strain. On Mawan Island, twenty-five miles by hydrofoil from Hong Kong, he wants to create another Hawaii. There are lovely beaches and the site for a super championship golf course. Also, as one would expect, there are problems. Nevertheless, with co-operation from the right quarters, it could come and it won't be Kim's fault if it doesn't.

Our visit to Fanling terminated, correctly, with good talk in the clubhouse. This is a delightful place. Glimpsed through the trees, it could well be a plantation mansion in one of the deep southern states of America. The building is white, terraced, colonnaded, and contains more golf trophies than I can remember having seen in any other club. In addition to novelties like a 'Best Average Cup'—which a humorist donated for the most consistently good scorer in the hottest month of the year—there is a 'Nil Desperandum' trophy, and more than a dozen 'Farewell' cups, presented by members on departure, in gratitude for happy times. The 50th birthday year was 1939 and on that occasion so many cups were donated that, allowing for two competitions each week, the year is not long enough!

I have briefly touched on the exciting history of the Royal Hong Kong Golf Club and now I find among my notes an extraordinary item. It appears that King George V agreed to be patron of the club in 1911. This royal favour continued until 1915, then, for some inexplicable reason, the patronage lapsed. Some amends were made in 1924 when H.R.H. Prince George, the Duke of Kent, became an Honorary Member.

For a weekend game of golf at Fanling the drill is to book or telephone for a time a week ahead. The draw is made, and starting times on the Old and New courses are published on Tuesday in the *South China Morning Post*. Golfers consult the newspaper to find out when they are off. This has become an accepted procedure and the couple of columns of starting times in a large-scale national newspaper is surely unique in golf.

Despite congestion, golf costs at Fanling are unusually low. Clubhouse accommodation is available at only 10s. a night; 6s for lunch; 7s. 6d. for an extremely good dinner.

Along with Peter Thomson, Dai Rees and other privileged people, I was enrolled as a 'Fanlingerer', an excellent charitable institution pledged to help the war blinded. You get a tie, and a booklet explaining that 'The Fanlingerer is a good-tempered, friendly animal, originally found in large numbers singing happy jingles in the vicinity of drink holes . . .'

CHAPTER SEVEN

Hong Kong Has a
Shangri-La

WE WERE INVITED to a party by the Skipper of the Royal Hong
Kong Golf Club, Colonel the Honourable 'Duggie' Clague at his
home among the parasol pines near Fanling.

Many golfing, and non-golfing, people sipped and chatted on
smooth lawns by the swimming pool. Economist Sir Joseph
Lockwood discussed with the Governor how free enterprise has
made for the great prosperity of Hong Kong. We were getting
into deep water so I reminded Lord Shawcross of a golf story he
once told at a '30 Club' dinner in London. Lady Shawcross doesn't
play. 'A toast to the other vices,' she said, raising her glass, and we
all went indoors to cold salmon, sucking pig and a dozen eastern
alternatives all worth coming from England to sample.

Duggie Clague has a mammoth group of Hong Kong businesses embracing everything from heavy industry to the large-
scale manufacture of artificial flowers. He also has a 'London
house' on the Sunningdale golf course. During the war he was
taken prisoner by the Japanese, escaped, and led guerillas. He was
one of the senior officers who took the surrender when the
enemy left the island. Once, 'just to take a look see', he returned
to Hong Kong Island under the enemy's nose and had a bathe in
Deep Water Bay.

With a bathe in mind in addition to golf, the Golf Widow and
I also went to Deep Water Bay. We had in store the pleasure of
hearing a senior professional talking of the old days. Deep Water
Bay is six miles from Hong Kong and costs only 8s. in one of the
fleet of taxis owned by Chinese golf addict, Mr Choy.

The golf club comes under the banner of Royal Hong Kong
and the maestro commanding is Bill Hitchens, a professional
golfer since 1910, when he worked in a London club-making

48

factory in East Sheen. After the 1914-18 war Bill became assistant at Richmond Park under J. H. Taylor's brother Josh. Then he came to the Royal Hong Kong club and without much doubt was the first British golf professional to be appointed in the Far East.

No-one in any walk of working life puts in more hours than the old senior golf pros and this applies to Bill. He lives on the Kowloon side of the water and leaves his home at about 6.30 a.m. to be at Deep Water at 8 o'clock. He seldom finishes before 8 o'clock in the evening and rarely takes a day off.

Deep Water Bay is a short, 9 holes course, less than 3,500 yards, twice round. More than once, Bill has done nine consecutive threes. He doesn't claim this as a tremendous golfing feat, but it is a couple of shots inside par and when it happens the lovely valley in which the course is set looks even more beautiful.

High hills, broken only with semi-skyscrapers perched on crags, arise on three sides and the entrance to the glen stretches down to a pleasant sandy beach. During the war, when the Japanese were in occupation, the clubhouse was used as a piggery, and going back further there were wild tigers and grey wolves. A python, eleven feet in length, was caught, stuffed and displayed in the bar. Also, ladies were wearing shorts on the course and I am wondering if this is the first instance of such frivolity in golf.

Deep Water Bay G.C. was always progressive. There was once a caddie-strike and 100 sepoys were sent over from the barracks to relieve difficulties. When the club became completely mechanised in 1927 the labouring water-buffaloes went, but in that year foxes became a nuisance. Also, Bernard Shaw visited the club.

'Hong Kong' is Chinese for 'Fragrant Harbour', but by far the most fragrant spot we visited on the island is the Shek O Country Club, just fourteen miles from the buzzing crowds who make money instead of honey.

Shek O is a sheltered, though not so secret valley. Twenty-one householders living there own the golf club (limited to 300 members), the swimming pool, such accoutrements as a small driving range, and an army of devoted club servants. There is considerable visitor restriction at the club; also, only twenty-one building sites are allowed on the estate. None of the rank and file membership has any say in the running of the club and that suits everyone, including the Shek O Development Company which owns the lot.

The Convenor (they don't have a President, Captain or Professional) is the executive boss, and his rule is absolute, benevolent and, of course, honorary. My buddy Graeme Nicholl is the Secretary. He reports to the Convenor (currently the genial Walter Vaughan, a past-captain of Royal Hong Kong), and he, old Uncle Tom Cobley and all, report to the chairman of the company.

The clubhouse, a simple bijou, is built on a peak looking down on the serene valley which is sheltered from the noisy world, and laid out as a charming golf course.

Because, here and there, rock comes to the surface, the lie of your ball could once be improved on the outward 9, but you can't improve the view.At all times the links is a short shot from the sea. At the 6th (Land's End) you have to carry a neck of ocean with your drive as at the renowned hole at Pebble Beach in California. The 18 holes stretch to about 5,000 yards, short enough, but so pleasant, particularly for the predominantly senior membership with corresponding avoir du pois.

The impression of playing in a lovely valley is constant. You are away from unpleasant things. Within minutes of arrival, the Golf Widow and I both said 'Shangri-la!' As for testing golf, don't expect too much. Kel Nagle holds the course record with 58 that can't last. But who cares.

The members of Shek O really rally round. Mr Nordahl Wallem (I hope he will excuse me for tossing in the fact that he is a Norwegian millionaire) has generously presented a new watering system, and someone else is giving a ski-lift to transport players from the 17th green to the lofty 18th tee. The bridges over burns are ships' plates from the docks . . . In fact, Shek O affluence is liberal in an unobrusive way.

One day, the Secretary was making a course inspection when he was accosted by a homely little chap. They passed the time of day, and the visitor said: 'Nice course you have here. My name's Joe Kraft and I'm from Chicago. I make cheese.'

Everyone who is anyone tries to take a peep at Shek O. Many of the twenty-one villas looking down on the valley are owned by the large Hong Kong companies and are used by their executives for entertaining. Jardine Matheson's have the one with the St Andrews flag, and a United States businessman has the 'Hanging Gardens of Babylon' that rises as a background to the 15th green.

Also, we met a very remarkable club servant.

The Belles of
Shek O
—

Mr Lau Kang Poo has been the Chief Steward at Shek O for more than a quarter of a century. But he is much much more. As Headman, or elder, of Shek O village he is a man of considerable importance. The village is a collection of houses on the promontory that juts out to sea. All the club staff come from there and Mr Lau engages them (indoor and outdoor), determines salaries, and takes any disciplinary action necessary. He has about a hundred people in his charge.

In a small basement room, an abacus on his table, he is clearly a man of substance. His son, like most of the young men from the village, is a steward on an ocean-going liner. But the girls in the village work as caddies and for them this is considered a high honour, quite unlike the state of affairs in the villages near Fanling, where the elders said to club officials: 'You have perverted our sons. You shall not have our daughters.'

The little girl caddies at Shek O are worth coming miles to see. Three of them were recently upgraded to 'special club assistants'. They are Kitty, Nancy and Julie (she wanted that name after Julie Andrews) and wear snappy tight blue pants, blue sleeveless tunics with brass buttons, white silk shirts with ritzy cuff-links, and pale blue bandeaux in their hair.

GRANNY CADDIE

Kitty conducts the charming 'Half Way House' by the 10th tee. Coloured tiles, geraniums, a miniature Chinese bridge ... Most attractive, like a chip from a willow-pattern plate—where you can get drinks.

These are little things, and Shek O is made up that way, with strong emphasis on homely privacy. There is a strong family side, and the swimming pool, with the professional 'save-lifer' (as the Chinese call him), serves the dual purpose of keeping the kiddies happy and away from the golf course.

Three times a week, Billy Tingle comes over from his Hong Kong duties to give swimming and athletic instruction. Billy is five feet one inch of bounding Yorkshire energy. How he ever persuaded the Hong Kong Cricket Club to lend him their sacred sward, bang in the centre of the city with a land value of £5,000,000, no-one will ever know. But the Hong Kong kiddies benefit there, because Billy puts them through his course of games and athletics. He has become a bi-weekly institution.

Every Boxing Day, and this has been going on at Shek O for years, golfers set off in sixes, each member of the 'team' carries one club, all different. On these occasions the tiny children of the village turn out to caddie. There have been as many as two hundred and eighty! Each gets a present, and it has been known for members to finish up by carrying their kiddie caddies!

Village life and the golf club are tightly interwoven. The Secretary told me he once had to visit the local school to report that some of the children had been playing on the course. He had serious talk with the school ma'am and with great dignity and good humour a settlement was made whereby there would be no further trespassing—in exchange for the present of a football!

There is no post office in the village; letters, which are rare, go for collection to the communal assembly room, where Mr Lau, the golf club Steward, is master. In the garden of the police station there is an emblem in enamelled clay of John Bull shaking hands with John Chinaman.

No starting times are ever necessary at Shek O golf. Only at weekends, when big business pauses, do the occupiers of the lovely villas escape from the city and come to re-charge their batteries in the lovely valley. Then things become crowded, in a bearable way. But normally everything at Shek O is leisurely. Since 1925 this is where the privileged few have relaxed. The first chairman of the company was named Bird and he chose the club motto which encircles the ibis bird and means "In the middle it is best you go'.

The Golf Widow and I left Shek O with much regret. The valley is very near to what every golf addict has in the back of his mind as a retreat for the day the football pools come up.

Hong Kong was an adventure, and meeting old and new friends was always enjoyable. Most importantly, the golf took us away from the bustling cities of Victoria and Kowloon, which frankly are not for us. Colourful Chinese people, fascinating junk life, thousands of small venturous restaurants . . . We could take all that. But, towering above everything, there are menacing skyscrapers of flats, office blocks, hotels (two of which are 300 feet tall), all terrifyingly clinical. Buzzing along crowded streets like demented bees, four million lost souls chase dollars. Frightful.

'Nothing in Hong Kong is quite as it appears to be. There's always something else, beneath the surface,' said Henry Heath. Of course he is right.

The British Colony started back in 1841. In those days the island had a bad reputation for ill-health, running sores, deafness and dysentery. All that has gone. Brainy British administration and Chinese hard work have produced a kind of twentieth century civilisation.

'It is a twenty-four hours slog,' said a Chinese businessman. 'I have to work much harder in Hong Kong than in China. But I know my son will get a good start,'

The Golf Widow's great-grandfather lived here, and when he eventually returned to Plymouth he brought back his pigtailed Chinese servant. The poor chap couldn't stand English crowds and climate, and pined until he was allowed to return to Hong Kong. To-day the reverse would happen. Unless, of course, he was a golfer living at Shek O.

CHAPTER EIGHT

Land of the Golfing Dragon

THE FORTUNE TELLERS in the Ginza area of Tokyo will inform you that there are good and bad days for doing anything. Aided by a combination of the twelve animals and the elements, astrologers, hand-readers, snake-charmers, faith-healers, and practitioners of the acupuncture art, are all available with advice on health and sports matters.

'The assurance is most gratifying that every day is good for golf,' said a Tokyo textile manufacturer who obeys his graphologist at least four times a week at the Kasumigaseki club.

'*Golf hyo*' is Japanese for 'golf addict'. 'Golf Widow' is accepted into the language as it stands, and this lonely race of women is becoming an increasing domestic problem.

In 1946 there were 17 golf courses in Japan; in 1966 there are about 400, but these figures only partly reflect the astounding growth of the game.

The Ginza is Japan's whirlpool of multi-racial restaurants, swanky shops, fragrant teahouses and smelly clip-joints. In this neighbourhood there are hundreds of *pachinko* salons. This craze for pin-table gambling is Japan's other post-war phenomenon.

But the big thing is golf, about which so much has already been written in Britain and America that I shall have difficulty in finding a new way to capture the immensity of the subject.

Figures don't mean a thing. In Britain—where we have golfed for at least three hundred years (compared to about sixty in Japan)—there are approximately $1\frac{1}{2}$ million golfers. As I write, there are at least 4,000,000 folk in Japan who call themselves golfers, and this figure may well be 5,000,000 by the time this book is in print.

Currently, only ten per cent. are club members because, unfortunately, private golf clubs are expensive and exclusive, and there are very few public courses and even these are too costly.

The head of the Japan Golf Association told me that it is quite impossible to print an accurate list of courses and locations because it would always be out of date. Golf clubs incubate at a fantastic rate, but because there is a driving range in every back garden and on almost every factory roof, golfers hatch out at a more alarming rate, and the question is whether there will ever be enough nests to keep them happy.

More than three quarters of Japan is steeply mountainous, yet in the remaining space this ingenious race have piled in paddy fields, great cities, and nearly 100,000,000 people, many of whom are pressing for more golf courses to satisfy inhuman hunger.

When we were there, in Tokyo alone there were more than 350 public driving ranges, and facilities for tuition and practice, and I would estimate there are the same number, in ratio to population, at Osaka, Kobe, Nagoya and the other big cities. Additionally, every large factory, block of offices and apartments have nets on the roofs wherein happy hackers can sweat and swear.

This teeming nation has recognised the limitless fun of golf at all levels. Later I shall tell of industrialists, geishas, minions and millionaires who play and enjoy an addiction more powerful than the poppy. But first a word about another aspect of golf in Japan.

In the land of the dragon, a golfer is like an Englishman who owns a Rolls Royce. When the Japanese hubby says goodbye to his children and strides off with his clubs on Saturday afternoon, he is knocking the Joneses for a six. Nippon neighbours peep through the slats of their blinds and go green with envy. No status symbol in Japan is comparable with golf.

Returning to where we started. In the Ginza, between the man who sells live baby turtles and a barber's shop, there is a stall from whence you can buy one of those useful shoulder bags which are given free (but only to first-class passengers) by all the international airlines. The selection offered for sale by this enterprising fellow ranges from the deep blue BOAC bag to the flashier red satchel with the PAN-AM signia. They are all there and the little shop does a lively business to folk who like to swank. Now, if you consider this a queer state of affairs, what do you think of the go-getting trader who, in some mysterious way, has acquired a selection of peak caps with badges from all the best golf clubs? They sell like hot cakes!

The foregoing will indicate what golf means in the Land of

Chen Chin Po
NATIONALIST CHINA
Tokyo

the Dragon. And while on dragons it should be remembered that here is no mystic symbol acceptable only to superstitious simpletons. In Japan, dragons are as real as golf. You can't see them, of course, but then you can't see the scent of cherry blossom. Dragons drift about golf courses in much the same way as they drift over rivers and they affect the golfer and angler alike. Just as they can put a fine fish on the hook so can they, with their sulphurous breath, blow a ball from the hole.

Addicts in Japan are affected by these things. One becomes pensive and before we were in the country more than a few hours I began to theorise. The Japanese are invariably good putters and I came to believe that I knew the reason. Buddhism is the acceptance of life and here I decided was the answer to good putting. The rest of the world miss four-footers and anger ruins the next

Yuji Kodera
of the
JAPAN GOLF
ASSOCIATION

two or three shots because of tension. My theory was that the Japanese (many of them being Buddhists) would accept the missed putt without pain or inward agitation. The player would immediately forget the trouble and sail on smoothly and peacefully. May I say quickly that this highfalutin theory of mine was bunk. Japanese golfers get as agitated as the rest of us. We played, or walked around, many courses in Japan and although we didn't notice a single club-thrower, I believe there is even more spiked-shoe dervish dancing on Japanese greens than we have in Europe or America.

So much for theorising. Now for facts.

Japan is mainly three large islands, swinging upwards south-west to north-east about 1,200 miles long by maybe 200 miles at the widest point. When we were there the population census was published and it is my guess that most of the 98,274,961 folk not only awake to the 7 a.m. television show 'Good morning, Golf!' and close down with 'To-day's Golf Hint' at 11.25 p.m., but they also intermittently ogle at Shell's Wonderful World of Golf, the Lloyd Mangrum-Betty Hicks show, the Palmer-Nicklaus-Player series, or the popular Chen Chin Po instructional programme. There are seven alternative T.V. channels in Japan, usually serving up thrice daily golf during twenty-four hours of viewing. In parenthesis, I would mention that when we were in Osaka, although there were serious production problems in industry, there seemed more concern because no arrangement had been made to televise the Bangkok Open Championship.

Japan has at least a dozen national magazines, or newspapers, for golfers, and all clubs (even municipal) have their own membership journals, some of which are printed in colour.

In this swarm of busy golf addicts, the caddies seem calm and serene. Mostly girls, they are well-trained, elegantly uniformed, and lodged in comfortable dormitories. At lush clubs the girls are even taught social graces, like cooking, flower decoration and the tea ceremony, so that they can maintain the high position which is their due when they marry and caddying comes to an end.

Regarding these matters I became knowledgeable at the Japan Golf Association, which is just above the Tokyo offices of Wells Fargo, and just about as incredible! According to popular television, Wells Fargo, like the Mounties, always 'get their man'. The Japan Golf Association are in the process of getting all their men, and women too, in the greatest corral of golfers ever known. Keeping accurate, up-to-the-minute tally of Japanese golfers is impossible. Mr Yuji Kodera, the executive director, generalises in round millions. Only an addict himself would want to care for this fast-growing octopus.

Mr Kodera learnt his golf on the campus at Princeton University, then he did a golf tour of England and Scotland. Then he returned and won the fine cup presented by the Prince of Wales when he visited Japan in 1922. Mr Kodera's handicap was then 3 and he was one of his country's back markers.

We discussed the mournful subject of ages and I told Mr Kodera mine. He said 'I can give you nine shots.' He doesn't look it.

Well, this is the man who is titular chief of Japanese golf and we couldn't have been luckier than to have him as our host on a visit to his favourite golf club.

But first we wanted to assess the range of Japanese golf, to have the full blast of contrast. From what we had read, we knew of the luxury product. I suspected that Mr Kodera's Sayama Club would be lush, so we first wanted a glimpse at the populo, where nine out of every ten Japanese golfers play when they visit a course, which is too seldom.

The 1966 Tokyo Open (gloriously won by Irishman Hugh Boyle) was played on two of the four golf courses owned by a Japanese newspaper. The press are throwing in their weight to further popularise golf in Japan—if that is possible—and during much of our tour the main sports paper *Hochi Shimbun* had assigned to me an interpreter guide. He took us to the Shiba driving range.

At this great centre there is accommodation for 150 golfers to drive from pens simultaneously, in three tiers (two under cover), from 6 o'clock in the morning until 11 o'clock at night. You pay 100 yen entrance fee (or you can get a book of 30 dozen tickets for 3,000 yen), 200 yen for hire of shoes and clubs, 250 yen for a basket of two dozen balls, and 400 yen for instruction lasting twenty minutes. There are 1,000 yen to the £.

In Japan the ranges are big business. At Shiba the permanent staff is one hundred and fifty assistants, working in shifts, and when we were there a team of new employees was going through a course of instruction.

In the cleaning room, we saw part of the stock of 180,000 golf balls with eleven men working in shifts, shovelling them into a launderette contrivance.

The up-picking is not done by vehicle with a scoop, as I have seen in the United States. Instead, dozens of young students come at the end of the day to earn cash—most of which goes right back for golf tuition!

We chatted with a geisha customer with a compact little swing and a pleasing simper. She proudly mentioned that the last Kanto Women's Championship had been won by a geisha in a sudden death play-off, after a tie with a previous Ladies Champion.

Golf swings at Shiba are sometimes extraordinary, but of the customers' keenness there is no doubt and this is stimulated in

Night session at
the SHIBA

The Shiba driving range

many ways by the promoters. Once Shiba owned a railway, but they sold out for golf and now own many ranges and golf courses.

We asked our interpreter, friendly Mr Iwata, to take us to 'a typical municipal club'. There are thirteen in Tokyo.

The Rokugo Golf Club is still in the capital, although it is at least five miles from the city centre. The track is dead flat, rather bald because of the tremendous traffic, surrounded by factories making cameras, textiles, chemicals ... And criss-crossed with canals, railways and part of the longest mono-rail in the world. The latter goes to and from the city centre to the airport and is only one of the distractions to what could never be peaceful golf.

My criticism must not be harsh. In any case, despite inclement weather, the endless stream of four-balls were having a wonderful time. As one would expect, the course is tight and fairways often cross, and tees are uncomfortably close to greens. In fact, the girl caddies (smart as usual, and in attractive uniforms with chevrons denoting years of service) wear crash helmets as protection. An American visitor said 'Golf balls rain down like bazooka shells!' The city authorities rightly protect their staff, although I didn't see any players in armour.

Each caddie pulls two trolleys and is paid 320 yen a player, making 15s. a round. You might call it danger money.

One would not describe the course either as stimulating or as a great test of golf, although the 3rd hole is a thrill. This is a dead straight 360 yards between two parallel overhead rail tracks not more than 50 yards apart which makes even professionals, for obvious reasons, sometimes take irons from the tee.

I know some golf courses in England and America which are similar to Rokugo, and it is an undeniable fact that here are the places where you find real golf enthusiasm. I might also mention that par figures are returned at Rokugo (scorecards are always taken) more often than in most clubs I visited in Japan, or in fact elsewhere.

Mr Kodera had said we would play Sayama 'if it doesn't rain', but I had a feeling that under his breath he was saying 'just try and stop me!' It was equally clear that my visit gave him some kind of excuse to get away from the avalanche of golf figures and correspondence relating to new clubs, and play his favourite course.

Sayama Golf Club is 35 miles from Tokyo, beautifully set in an important tea-growing area. 'Sayama' means narrow mountain, but there are no mountains to climb, only gentle slopes winding between pretty trees and skilfully placed bunkers. There are 27 holes and these can be played by choosing on the 1st tee the two nines you intend.

Yuji Kodera laid out the early nine holes and helped to get the Club started in 1959. It is his baby and although he has done his stint as President and Captain, he retains the job as Convenor of the Greens Committee because the general upkeep of the course is his passionate concern. Fof this reason *he regularly plays with his head greenkeeper because he says 'How can a man become dedicated and knowledgeable if he doesn't play?'*

This most commendable practice, which may be the answer to universal greenkeeper problems, is revolutionary in Japan, where the division between members and club employees is possibly wider than elsewhere.

On Japanese courses there are nearly always two separate greens of equal quality alongside each other on every golf hole. This is to ensure that one is in good playing condition while the other is being dressed or fertilised. Yuji Kodera, a purist, doesn't believe in this idea because approach shots can be spoilt. He won't have any of this lark at Sayama. Instead, he arranged that work on the greens is done in two halves, as in Britain. The 'winter half' is *bent* grass, and the 'summer half' *korai* grass.

Along with Head Greenkeeper Aoki, the other member of our four-ball was Singo Hama, a 'leftie', who also happens to be the Editor of *Golf*, the Japanese monthly magazine which undeniably shows the way to any similar publication in Britain or America.

We crashed along, employing the same angry expletives and hoots of joy that are common in all lands which cater for happy hackers.

In Japan, or elsewhere, golf is a great leveller.

CHAPTER NINE

Escape to Harihan

KATSUJI YABUKI OF TOKYO is a contemporary searcher into the arts of our great game. He has joined a club which is one hour by car from the capital, near his home at Kawasaki City. To Katsuji I am indebted for supplying the following information regarding the more sordid side of Japanese golf. I mean the cost.

One must never confuse costs with values. It seldom follows that because something is·expensive it is therefore good; nor are cheap things necessarily bad. For example, in Scotland where golf is the best, it is usually cheap.

A twenty-five guineas annual golf subscription can be dear, or dirt cheap, depending on how often the member plays. The foolish fellow who goes around the course only two or three times a year is paying heavily for his golf, whereas I get my addiction almost for nothing because I play at least four rounds a week.

Against this background, let us review the case of Mr Yabuki, new member of the Chigasaki Golf Club. Nine holes by the sea; a pleasant, unostentatious club which a retired businessman would join for economical fun at the time of life when he has to pay for what he gets from his own pocket, entertainment expenses having dried up.

The Chigasaki Club is not a Wentworth, Royal Wimbledon, Coombe Hill, Westchester Country Club or Bel Air. Compare it with Sydenham, Tyrrell's Wood and dozens of others around London, or perhaps with Fairfax, near Washington, or Evanston, near Chicago. You don't join Chigasaki for luxury, but you do get a good game of golf among nice chaps.

Having been correctly introduced, Mr Yabuki paid an entrance fee of 340,000 yen, equivalent to £340. This was rather higher than the specified rate because the membership was complete and he had to buy a 'transfer' from a retiring member. This traffic in

65

memberships is customary, and widows expect to show a sound profit on what their husbands originally paid to join a club.

Mr Yabuki's annual subscription is only £8. Unfortunately, it does not end there. Each time he plays, a 'green fee' is paid. This covers the government tax, the staff welfare contributions, and a compulsory payment towards the upkeep of the road leading to the club. The green fee for members is customary in Japan and always covers the three items mentioned. So, each time he plays, over and above his annual subscription, Mr Yabuki pays about 15s. Additionally, his caddie costs him 2s. 6d. for nine holes.

Because of crowding, guests are discouraged, particularly at weekends. The 'visitor's fee' for 9 holes is 25s. on weekdays, and 35s. at weekends, plus 40 per cent for each additional nine holes.

Some private clubs in the provinces, like the Sapporo Golf Club on Hokkaido Island, or the Nagasaki Country Club, cost less than Chigasaki, but a great number cost more. As an example: at the Kasumigasaki Golf Club, near Tokyo, where Pete Nakamura and Koichi Ono suprised the world by beating Sam Snead, Jimmy Demaret, Peter Thomson, Gary Player, etc., in the 1957 Canada Cup, an introduced visitor costs his host £3.10.0 on weekdays, and £5 at weekends and holidays.

But the really diamond-studded affair is the '300 Club', near

Yokohama. This was started by a man named Noboru Goto, head of a large firm with interests in departmental stores, railways and what not. Only the presidents of companies, or very senior citizens, are admitted here. Entrance fee: 3,000,000 yen (£3,000), with other items in the same ratio. For every game of golf a member plays he is about £10 out of pocket (before he has a beer and sandwich) over and above his annual subscription. The girl caddies at the 300 Club are chosen like mannequins.

In my humble opinion—shared, I am glad to say, by many serious Japanese golfers—finance is the one aspect that blights this exciting, vibrant world of Japanese golf. Maybe the limited number of courses and the astonishing demand make inflation inevitable. Nevertheless, your old-fashioned addict will never reconcile cash and extravagance with the simple joys of democratic golf with a small bag.

Many of the golf club memberships in Japan have been bought up by big companies and corporations for their executives to use for business entertaining. This type of corporate membership, after a few years, is considered a company asset. By buying a 'block', the entrance fees may be only £600 each, instead of £750, and it is not unusual for a company to sell off some of their memberships at a big profit.

While we were in Japan, a new golf club was inaugurated and at the party there was an old lady. She was asked whether she played. 'No,' she said, 'I'm not a golfer. I bought membership purely as an investment two years ago when they first decided to start the club. I have just sold out at twice the price of my participation.' Before a single ball had been hit!

To digress for just forty-eight hours.

Having golfed ourselves to near stupification in India, Thailand, Hong Kong and Tokyo, the Golf Widow and I resolved to sit back in provincial Japan to contemplate, not our navels, but our notes which were the quickly recorded impressions of a tour heavily laden with interest and fact. We wanted to see if we could read our scribble before we filled more notebooks.

First we had to let the machine run down, to relax. One way is to take a Turkish bath and in Japan this kind of thing has been brought to a fine art.

During our trip around Ireland we found one Maggie Daly, in Ballybunion, who supplies hot seaweed baths to revive wilting golfers. The contrast between Maggie's humble establishment on the beach in County Kerry and the public bathing facilities in Japan is considerable—although it may be difficult to decide which bath does most good.

O-furo means 'honourable bath' and you can take one in dozens of different Tokyo establishments, either alone or with others; hot or cold; unadulterated; or with sulphur, milk, lemon or hormones. Your bath can be vitaminised, irradiated, electric, soporific, or aphrodisiac. It can be Japanese, Turkish, Finnish, or Roman; with or without attractive female attendants, either in vests and shorts, or in the nude. Afterwards, you may take inhalations, sprays, showers, or sun-lamp treatment.

All this you learn from the pamphlet with English translations, available at the door and which is read avidly before taking the plunge. There is plenty of choice, and you can guess which the Golf Widow and I sampled. Enough to know that it prepared us for work, before sneaking off to the peace of a provincial Japanese. Inn.

Looking back on our journeyings, my wife had two big laughs. One was at Hirono where, before a dozen Japanese who were waiting to see the distinguished British golf writer perform, I put two successive drives into the lake. The other occasion was when a girl named Hanna insisted on scrubbing my back at the Harihan Inn.

Not for a moment do I imagine that we explored ground unknown to all British golf addicts. But these things were new to us and we were so enthralled that I shall set it all down so that you can either read on, or skip the remainder of this chapter and join up with the golf later.

We took the Tokeido Express, reputedly the fastest train in the world, which runs to split-second timing from the capital to Osaka, a distance of about three hundred miles.

To secure places on this magnificent train you either book days ahead, or you get some kind soul at the Japan Travel Bureau to pull strings, which we did. And the least I can do in return is to say with great sincerity that neither in Europe nor the United States have I travelled on land in such comfort, so quickly.

There are many pleasant touches. Following a gentle carillon of bells, a tannoyed voice in Japanese, then English, gives regular information of interest to the traveller; a telephone is available for businessmen who can't give their Tokyo offices three hours and ten minutes peace, and I was informed that I could have 'phoned my home in England without the slightest trouble; light meals and drinks are constantly offered by young ladies who push trolleys up and down the wide gangway; when the inspector has seen all the tickets, before leaving he stands at the end of the coach, doffs his hat, bows, and says 'thank you'.

Between Tokyo and Osaka the train stops twice, at Nagoya (large, industrial and rather ugly), and Kyoto, where there are many temples, including the lovely Shimo-Gamo shrine, alongside the lovely Shimo-Gamo golf range.

From the train we had full view of the economical use of land. Every flat patch is a paddy field, or a tea plantation, and in rocky places there are orange groves and vegetables. Mounting upwards towards the high mountains are the playgrounds where the Japanese go for summer vacations. The land is good only for climbing and golf. For those lucky enough to have the necessary cash, there await some of the most beautiful courses in the world.

To the left of the rail track is Mount Fuji, and what a sight it is! A 7th-century Japanese poet said:

> *The clouds of heaven dare not cross it,*
> *Nor the birds of the air soar above.*

Nevertheless, in the foothills, these tremendous Japanese have laid out seventeen golf courses. These are not '9 hole goat tracks'. Not a bit of it. They are long 18 holes of swinging golf (nearly every course over 6,500 yards), greens often cut into mountain sides, and fairways penetrating fearlessly into forests of fir and pine.

We reached Osaka on the dot, and the little porters in red jockey caps and black plus-fours bustled around, anxious to help us on to the next stage of our journey.

From Osaka to Kobe is thirty miles of almost continuous city; then we motored up a long winding hill for an hour, until the car stopped. A Japanese friend had made the arrangements, advised the inn-keeper of our approximate arrival time, and as our vehicle approached, a door opened in a high wall and a man emerged to take our bags. We entered, the door closed, and we were in a new world.

Japanese inns, *ryokans*, are not usually frequented by foreign visitors, which is a pity, for they give the rest which is so necessary after gadding about in Tokyo.

Two pleasant girls in kimonos were at my elbow, beckoning me into an attractive, enclosed glade, with streams, waterfalls, bridges and the inevitable trees with twisted trunks and flat tops. After the city noises of Osaka and Kobe, this was never-never land!

As was proper, the girls (our private servants during the stay)

led me gently up a path, leaving the Golf Widow to follow at a respectful distance.

The Harihan Inn comprises a cluster of small, self-contained chalets around the main building, where men go to drink *sake*, smoke and play mahjong; and where the communal bathroom is available for the women. Each chalet is perched on a little peak, nestling among cherry trees, with a small terrace overlooking the glade. All rather phoney, but daintily decorative, and each chalet designed for privacy. Ours had a large salon wherein we ate and slept (on the floor, of course), a kind of ante-room where the serving girls attended to our clothes and minded their own

business, and two lovely sun loggias, one out of doors overlooking flowers and a little waterfall; the other behind glass so
that occupants can enjoy the garden in cold weather. Also we
had a dressing room, a bathroom with a deep wooden bath sunk
into the floor, and, elsewhere, the usual offices.

The walls were mostly sliding panels of fine polished wood;
the only decoration was a single rose in a slim vase standing in
the *tokonoma*, which is the name given to the corner of honour
and which is usually the background for a favoured guest. The
one discordant bit of nonsense—a television set.

For meals we sat on cushions at the low table, although there
were western chairs in the loggias. The sun was bright and warm
and the world was smiling peacefully.

The Innkeeper came to pay his respects and to give small
presents: a table cloth and a fan for me, and a brochure about
the inn for the Golf Widow. I bowed and gave him a cigar which
he accepted with another bow, took two puffs without removing
the band, then laid it aside.

All this was correct and looked good, I assure you. For on
arrival, the serving girls had stripped us off and we were now
dressed in the proper Japanese clothes. The Golf Widow looked
magnificent in a patterned *yakata* with a sash and a big bow on
her behind; I wore a similar garment without the bow, and felt
like Chou Chin Chow in his underpants. But it was all good,
interesting stuff which would take us away from golf for a while
and freshen up our working ideas.

Hanna, serving girl No 1, brought us marzipan confections,
called *nama-gashi* and in a long unnecessary conversation she indicated that she would shortly serve a meal. Neither she nor her
mate had one single word of English, but the Golf Widow and
I had discussed the matter and had decided on a food preference.

'Suki-yaki,' I said firmly.

Hanna giggled, hissed (a sign of respect), bowed, and gave
instructions to her assistant.

The suki-yaki was a brilliant performance, with Hanna cooking at table in the approved fashion. There were thin slices of
meat, small Japanese onions, mushrooms, root vegetables,
shredded cabbage, squares of *tofu* (a custard-like Yorkshire pud-
ding), and half-a-dozen sauces.

During the actual devouring of the meal I had Hanna's undivided attention. After the nice bits of meat had been dipped in raw egg and fried, she popped them into my mouth with chopsticks. One could see she was a beautifully trained, top-level serving wench. Although she attended to my needs, like sponging hands and wiping my mouth, she also kept a watchful eye to see that the Golf Widow was also getting some food.

This was fine. There is nothing so pleasant as being pampered a bit after weeks of bruising from the golf game.

The meal ended, the gels cleared away, and without consultation laid out the big bed. Hanna put her hands against her cheek in the slumber attitude and pointed to the bed, then hastily ran off presumably in case I misconstrued her meaning.

After the siesta, the Golf Widow and I looking, no ' doubt, like a couple of extras from *The Mikado*, strolled in the garden. Then we watched suma wrestling on the television. Folk who think golfers look batty should see an incredibly fat man stamping about before his suma battle, tossing sawdust over himself to drive off the evil spirits!

Time passed, and soon Hanna and her sidekick were rustling up another oriental banquet for Papa-san and Mama-san (as they called us), then it was bed again.

The lamp was on the floor alongside my pillow. I could very easily have got on with some work, but I settled for a glance through the publicity brochure about the Harihan Inn.

Even on arrival, we realised that this was no humble Japanese tavern, although when we decided on the escape plan we had simplicity in mind. The arrangement for us to stay at Harihan had been made by an influential Japanese friend, so it was quite by accident that we had come to this place of great luxury.

In modest English, the booklet said: 'Harihan, started as a restaurant in 1879 . . . is the choice of Japan's elite, including the Emperor and Crown Prince. To stay at the inn you must be introduced. The servant who waits on you has been intensively schooled to anticipate your every wish and to perform services with unobtrusive perfection. The Inn has been built with infinite attention to every detail, designed to delight the eye . . .

'Harihan's luxury is the oldest tradition. Even 85 years ago the toilet was of marble with a silver seat . . .'

Of course we wanted to stay on a while. I was just getting accustomed to sitting on the floor, having my back scrubbed, being fed and all the other little refinements which men enjoy in Japan. But elsewhere there was a job to do and by taking off my *yakata* and pulling on my trousers I indicated to Hanna that it was time for us to go. The girls expressed regret in the profuse way they had been trained, and Hanna reported our intention to the manager.

How could anyone question, or even scrutinise an hotel bill which is accompanied by this printed message. 'Many thanks for your stay at the Harihan Inn. May I ask you to sign your name on this card? I will preserve it for long in memory of your stay here and expect to take statistics of foreign tourist'.

Signed: The Manager.

I am not clear what is meant by 'statistics of foreign tourist', but one can be quite certain that the phrase is intended to bring happiness.

CHAPTER TEN

How Golf Started in Japan

THE BEST WAY to inspect any golf course is to get the Skipper to take you on a personally conducted tour. We did that at Kobe—in belting snow!

The Kobe Golf Club is about 3,000 feet up on the top of the Rokko Mountain. At the beginning of the century, golfers used to be carried ten miles from Kobe by palanquin! The course is closed for about five months each year because of inclement weather. But in mid-summer, when the city swelters in 90°, Rokko must be paradise.

The Captain, Mr Seiichi Takahata, had arranged for the care-taker to open up the Clubhouse, and when we arrived there was a great log fire crackling in the lounge; all the early records, plan of the course, and photographs, were laid out for our inspection.

Every Japanese golfer, all the 4,000,000 of them, should make the pilgrimage to the summit of Mount Rokko, because that is where it all started, in 1903, with the Kobe Golf Club.

At 3 o'clock in the afternoon of May 24th, a non-golfer named Hattori Ichizo swiped at, and by good fortune hit, a gutty ball, thus declaring the first golf course in Japan to be officially open. Mr Ichizo's performance was a jolly good show. We all know the ordeal of driving off before a crowd, but on an occasion such as this, it required real courage—particularly for a man whose only previous attempt to hit a stationary ball was at billiards.

I do not suppose that the Governor of the Hyogo Prefecture realised that by getting golf started in the Kobe district he was virtually cutting the first sod in a country which one day would go wild about the game. It is comforting to know that behind the Kobe scheme there was an Englishman. But we will come to him later.

First, I must tell of the reigning Captain of the Kobe Golf Club. For our introduction I am indebted to a friend who described

Mr Seiichi Takahata as 'one of the most revered men in Japan'. I am sure this is so. Not only did he establish the administration for golf in his country (based on the English Golf Union), find the site for Japan's best golf course, but also, in 1933, he managed to make the final of the Japanese Amateur Championship. I might also add that he is one of Japan's leading industrialists, extremely pro-British, and very kind.

From an international point of view, Mr Takahata has made his mark on golf more specifically than in the ways so far mentioned. This will be news to most people. Without a fragment of doubt—all aspects have been checked—Takahata was the man to invent covers for wooden clubs. It came about this wise.

While in England as a young man, Takahata lived in Kensington. He was a member of Addington, regularly played with Ted Ray at Oxhey, and when the Crown Prince' of Japan came to England, Takahata golfed him around and got him so keen that when he returned to Tokyo he had two courses built in the centre of the city. During this time, Takahata commissioned Jack Ross, the Addington professional, to make him a driver. So lovely, in the eyes of the young Japanese art lover, was this piece of polished persimmon that, rather than risk scratching the head of the club, Takahata asked a lady friend to make a protective covering. This prototype was knitted in heavy yellow yarn and attracted great attention from fellow members at Addington who promptly followed suit and got their ladies working.

The club covers soon became items of more than local interest. Disbelieving that anything so obvious had not previously been thought of, Takahata had enquiries made in New York, Chicago, Washington and Seattle, where his firm had offices. Exhaustive enquiries confirmed that covers for wooden clubs were unprocurable, unnecessary and totally unrealistic—commercially. No such objects existed in the United States. The quest continued in Scotland, and in the provinces of England, but always the answer was the same.

This was in 1916 when the world was at war. Not until the late 'twenties were club covers manufactured and sold by Arthur Bryant, and in St Andrews at the Tom Morris shop. Soon they were stocked everywhere.

Credit where credit is due. The Japanese are great bulk producers at lowly cost, but we usually say that the original article comes from the west. Well, this time a Japanese showed the way and if you think it is a small affair, it may be news that the annual sale of wooden club covers in Britain alone is estimated at 250,000.

In Japan, Mr Takahata has done more for golf than anyone. Like every serious golfer, he loves the best aspects but fears the worst of the great wave of fanaticism which is sweeping his country. When we were there he celebrated his seventy-ninth birthday, played with me on the best two courses in Western Japan, and took me to the Kwansei Golf Union, which controls 98 clubs in the area.

The knowledgeable Secretary of the K.G.U. showed me two interesting documents: a photograph of the Crown Prince of Japan playing against the Prince of Wales, Tokyo, 1922; and an old drawing of a Japanese warrior swinging a two-handed sword with a Harry Vardon grip!

But to return to Mount Rokko and the Kobe Golf Club with Skipper Seiichi. The caretaker produced the list of the 153 original members when the club started in 1903. From their names we gathered that they were practically all British, but also there was a sprinkling of Japanese, French and Germans. The club record boards show that although the first club champion in 1903 was a Scot named J. Adamson, no Briton has been champion since 1935. All are Japanese, which, of course, is as it should be.

We studied the booklet about the club and the scorecard. Everything at Kobe is in English and the atmosphere of the clubhouse positively breathes British golf. You could well be in Scotland! There is a photograph of Tom Morris Senior (a gift from Takahata) and all the oddments one finds in an old-established homely clubhouse; even a couple of Lawson Wood prints, an old cap, and a bag of derelict clubs left in a corner of the locker-room . . .

On the handicap sheet there are still a few British names, like Robertson, husband and wife, handicaps 3 and 16. Addicts, I bet. But the *pièce de resistance* in the Kobe clubhouse is the large photograph on the main wall of the lounge. It depicts a very English Englishman, comfortably confident, portly, heavy moustache, wearing white plus-fours, a panama hat, and carrying what looks like library books under one arm. Foot crossed, he leans on an unrolled umbrella.

This is Arthur Groom, founder of the club, the English merchant, who first opened the door and let the crowds in to Japanese golf.

Groom was comfortably well off, married to a Japanese lady, and without any doubt he was an energetic golfer who, these days, would be described as dynamic. With aid from a friend named R. Hartshorn, in twelve months he actually uprooted fifty big trees, and laid out four holes, then quickly another five, and by 1904 there were eighteen holes actually in play. And all this on a most unpromising site at the top of a mountain!

Because of circumstances, ours was a cursory visit. Next time (we have been invited to stay in Mr Takahata's summer villa on the mountain top) we shall play there.

The actual design of the course has undergone many changes since the early days, but the character can't alter. As with all mountain courses difficulties abound. Because of the snow storm we couldn't explore in detail, but there is a fine switch-back fairway, returning to the clubhouse from the back of beyond, and I am told the course is 'exciting'.

In 1912 a stone was erected on the summit of Rokko commemorating Arthur Groom's achievement. A worthwhile shrine. But I like to think of a little thing which the creator himself established to perpetuate his memory. The first hole at Kobe is named 'Dumpie', because that was Groom's favourite brand of whisky!

We did not find the Japanese cities outstandingly attractive. O. D. Russell, an American, described them as 'Wonderful, hybrid, dissolute, noisy, quiet, brooding, garish, simpering, silly, contemplative, cultured, absurd . . .' This covers everything. Enough to say, the prospect of visiting the Ibaraki Country Club after industrial Kobe and bustling Osaka was very sweet. Here, we had been told, Japanese golf is at its charming best. Now we were in the green again, among the forests, hills and beautiful lakes, and to make things even more attractive I was playing with Mr Fujii, the Manager of the club, and a very fine golfer.

My caddie was a kindly, motherly soul named Mrs Ogita and if I find myself repeatedly writing about caddies this is because I am nearly always lucky in having the aid of nice, chatty people. Mrs Ogita was no exception. Although she must be my age, in addition to pulling my heavy bag, she insisted on pushing me up the hills!

Mrs Ogita wanted to have conversation, but her English consisted only of a few golfing terms like 'Gu sha' (good shot) and 'Ba lu' (bad luck). I may say that in our game she used the latter the more often. However, she did know the numbers on the clubs, and using the long irons, plus simple signs, information was exchanged that we have families of two daughters and three sons, respectively.

The girl caddies at Ibaraki, as one would expect at a swanky club, are unusually smart. They wear tight brown pants, bright yellow windcheaters with green shoulder patches, white shoes, red socks, and the usual white cowl as protection from the sun. The girls (there are women too) are issued with four suits a year, and although the wages are good, most of them augment their fees by knitting wooden-club covers for the members.

Like the other 'girls' (150 caddies are dormitoried at Ibaraki), Mrs O. carries a little bag of seeded soil and a trowel. This is to repair her patrons' divot scars, a practice which has been adopted throughout Japan because, in fact, the turf does not divot but crumbles, so the replacing rule does not apply.

The courses at Ibaraki are laid out between gentle slopes,

Caddie
'MIA'
Ibaraki C.C.
——JAPAN

wooded knolls and picturesque lakes. Each hole on both courses is splendidly private and one has the impression that there is ample room without skimping. We played nine holes on the 'East', then nine on the 'West'. They are both fine tests with subtle gradients and a wide variety of hazards, natural and man-made. The 'East', opened in 1925, is 6,756 yards, and can be stretched to 7,000 yards for championships. The 'West' was opened in 1961, is shorter, and less dificult.

In the opinion of Mr Fujii, the best long holes are the 16th and 18th on the East course. But possibly the main terror is the short 14th on the West, where the tee shot must hit the green 180 yards away, or be engulfed, either in a lake, or in one of six cavernous bunkers.

Ibaraki is prosperous, sophisticated golf, under dedicated

79

direction. Someone has an eye to the future, for hundreds of young Caribbean pine trees have been skilfully planted to increase the fun for players in 1980 and onwards.

The wind blew unkindly from the north, so the shallow charcoal fires in the shelters were particularly comforting. Just a detail, but how pleasant to have tea, meat extract and coffee, all piping hot, instead of the usual Coca-Cola.

The charming Miss Sugimoto, lady Club champion, was pointed out to me at the practice nets. She was smart and very 20th century. An elderly Japanese gentleman who had joined me shook his head with a sad little smile as two other ladies in tight trousers and form-showing sweaters hurried past.

'Our country changes,' he said.

CHAPTER ELEVEN

Hirono, Talk, and a Mild Rebuke

OUR LAST GREAT TREAT was a visit to Hirono, without any doubt the best golf course in Japan.

It would be fair to say that Hirono has done much to bridge the gap between the Orient and the Occident, because this golf course is the result of close co-operation between a Japanese and an Englishman. The particular Japanese gentleman who dedicated himself to the task was our mentor and friend, Seiichi Takahata. He found the site and commissioned a great British golf-course architect to come out and draw up the plans. These early documents I have seen; they are the work of C. H. Alison, a Lancastrian who played for Oxford University at the beginning of the century, and has the distinction, in a 'varsity match, of once playing a shot from the roof of the Woking clubhouse!

That is the type of adventurous architect Takahata sought out to design the great golf course he had in mind.

At the risk of being accused of too frequently dipping into the past, I will do it again. Viscount Kuki was a distinguished sportsman; he was also a wealthy landowner who indulged an annual caprice by taking a party of friends for a mushroom-picking picnic. This regular romp took place on the part of his estate which Takahata coveted for a golf course. The friends talked the matter over, and eventually a company was formed, land purchased, and Hugh Alison sent for.

The first captain of the Hirono Golf Club was Seiichi Takahata, and he held the post for fourteen successive years. Now he is President.

I have been looking up the early story of Pine Valley, the famous golf club in the United States. There are many similarities with Hirono. For example, the piece of land which Takahata

81

F

found in 1932 was not unlike the famous 184 acres which the late George Crump discovered near Clementon, New Jersey, in 1912, and which he ultimately christened Pine Valley.

Although financial appreciation was the last consideration, both men chose well. Pine Valley land has multiplied fifty times in value and the same can be said of Hirono, which at present is worth at least £800,000. Comparison goes further. Colt laid out Pine Valley; and Alison, who designed Hirono, was his business partner.

Hirono is near the village of Miki, about twenty miles from the city of Kobe, and when you drive through the very handsome portals of the club you realise you are somewhere. There are even palms in the grounds, while snow is deep on Mount Rokko only twenty miles away. Every five years, by agreement of all parties, the Japanese Open Championship is held here, and there are those who say that since this is the best course in Japan the event should always be held at Hirono.

Like Pine Valley, Hirono is attractively timbered, also there are many lakes, in fact six holes (three in each half) have water involved. At one, the 5th, I put up an astonishing performance—even for me. This is a short hole, called 'Fiord' for an obvious reason. The distance from the tee is only 150 yards. Behind the driving ground, a chalet shelter copes with the usual hold-up and on this occasion there was an accumulation of four-balls (with their caddies) watching when I performed. A simple shot with a 4-iron was all that was required. Yet my ball plopped among the carp. I teed up another. Ever the optimist, I felt that an ace would completely make up for the initial tragedy, and restore me as an expert in the eyes of the beholders. Well, tragedy happened again. There was deathly silence, excepting for the splash, then the Golf Widow said 'Oh!'

I was so ashamed. Being a sympathetic golfer of great experience, Takahata knew how I felt. 'Dont' play another,' he said, softly, 'we have an interesting alternative.'

The others drove off, satisfactorily, and we all took the footpath around the lake, and up the wooded path to the green. Because one cannot 'play around' the lake, there is a second teeing ground (with a two stroke penalty) about thirty yards from the green on the safe side, for the craven who knows when he is beaten.

'I'll let this hole pass,' I said, getting out of sight from the crowd on the tee.

I got bogeys at the 6th, 7th and 8th, felt better, then, to get back to form, just slipped in a quick 7 at the 9th . . .

About 200 mixed staff, indoor and outdoor, maintain the Hirono Golf Club. Additionally, there are 150 girl caddies living in club dormitories, and casual labour is engaged to augment the greens staff as required. Many of the holes at Hirono remind me of Rosemount, Blairgowrie, my favourite course in Scotland, and as we went on our pleasant way, Seiichi told me about what we were seeing. Each hole was his child and he had cared for them all from birth, watching them develop, changing slightly (as golf has changed) from the original intention of their British parent.

The holes have been named picturesquely, often with wit. The 1st is 'Mount Okko' (male), because you can see it in the distance; graves from an old battlefield make natural bunkers to the right of the fairway on the 2nd, so the hole is 'Twin Barrows'; the 9th is 'Clubward Ho!'; the 10th is Mount Mekko (female); the 12th and 13th are named Pebble Beach and Pine Valley for obvious reasons, so is Quo Vadis, the 14th. The 13th was originally named 'Loch Lomond' but a committee made the change and I suspect it rankles a little with Takahata. Practically every hole is different in character and I cannot remember ever having played a more entertaining course, although, for the likes of me, it is difficult to get respectable figures. I suppose the most testing holes are the 15th (555 yards) and the short 7th (190 yards)—a death or glory hole if ever there was one.

We returned to the clubhouse for post mortems and the very first thing I saw was the large tapestry. Made in *petit point* after months of labour by the lady embroiderers of Kyoto, now embellishing this most unlikely setting, is the famous old picture 'Golfers, St Andrews, 1847'. It was produced at the special command of Takahata from a print he acquired during a visit to the Scottish home of golf.

In the locker room there was great jubilation for news had come through that Tadashi Kitta, the club professional, had just won the Open Championship of Thailand in competition with Peter Thomson and the other top professionals competing in what is called the Far East circuit. Kitta had often caddied for Takahata, so our friend was particularly delighted and told us of the dedicated young man who hits the ball incredible distances and is only 110 lbs. in weight. I asked how he did it and Takahata said that he had sought the answer to that sort of question all his life and doubtless would still be searching in the hereafter.

Before settling for serious talk we checked that our clubs were safely packed in the car. Caddie-masters in Japan usually give you a stringed label for attaching to your bag. This gives the number of clubs and the name of the caddie. Pilfering is unlikely but, like many other things, this detail illustrates the meticulous way the Japanese tackle golf. The fundamentals of the game can't change, but it is interesting to see how varying national characteristics have influenced normal routine. For example, I had never previously seen the caddie (not the player) marking the position of the ball when it interferes with the opponent's play. In Japan the caddie often uses a tiny wisp of red wool which she carefully places to give the exact position of the ball.

Before our whiskies, good hot green tea was served in the usual small cups without handles and these were filled up four or five times by the steward who was never far away from the President's table.

In Britain, a comforting stoop of ale is balm to the tortured golfer, but at the 19th hole in Japan first of all it is tea. My friends reminded me that the national beverage has a similarity to golf.

For two thousand years the Japanese have accepted *cha-do* (the way of tea), and this has not only philosophical dignity but, like golf, it is also an addiction. Without any doubt the beverage is an analytical passion combined with warm brotherhood, and of course golf is the same. Someone said 'In the hands of foolish persons the tea ceremony degenerates into a meaningless formality . . .' Does this not remind you of the oaf who only plays golf when 'he has the time', then usually with his trousers tucked into his socks?

As one would expect in the club with the best golf course, Hirono has some fine players. In his day, Takahata was one, and I know he is saying that his name appears too frequently in this book. But also it appears among the club honours, in fact too often to mention. Also, there is the name of A. G. Soto, who was the Japanese Amateur Champion and Hirono Club Champion for sixteen years (if we allow him his title during the non-

The 5th
Hirono
Japan.

'Fiord', at Hirono

golf war years), and I would like to know who, of any nationality, has a similar record.

Yet, among the giants, it is pleasant to regard the small fry who seldom win the silverware. Often at Hirono, although it is more popular at smaller clubs, members play for bars of chocolate. I heard of a club near Tokyo where this has become quite a craze. Play is for points on each hole and these are added up when the round is completed. Payment must be made in bars of chocolate purchased at the club shop and it is not unusual for a good player to leave for home with four or five dozen tokens of victory. In fact, golf widows and kiddies have become accustomed to welcoming daddy with 'How many bars have you won for us to-day?'.

In Japan these fads spread quickly. The Japanese have a passion for *imamekashi*, which means 'the very latest thing', and I have the impression that sellers of golf gimmicks, like putting spectacles, and such like, do big business.

But if you have in mind to make a fortune this way, remember that you are trading with a superstitious race. Not so prevalent around the big cities, but at provincial clubs, golfers most carefully watch their step. For example: Japanese players hesitate to carry a 4 wood, or even a 4 iron; the figure 4 is avoided as we avoid 13, because in Japanese *shi* means 4, and it also means 'death'. When unfastening his windcheater, the Japanese golfer never lets the right side flap over the left; this is bad luck and if it happens short putts will surely be missed that day.

All this is taken seriously. On the other hand, the Japanese have a great capacity to deal frivolously with some serious things. Daruma-san is the great Buddhist saint. A popular song goes: 'Daruma-san, Daruma-san, arrange for a fine day to-morrow so that father can go to golf and I can buy myself a pretty geisha'.

And so, as you may well have imagined, in the clubhouse lounge we reached the whisky stage, and if you don't believe the Japanese know about whisky, read this translation of the advertisement for a local brew: 'A magnificent whisky, pot-distilled of golden kanto barley and crystalline artesian water. Aged in sherry-cured oak, in a cool, silvery valley where even the scenery makes delightful drinking-in. Enjoy this piquant beverage in the after-dinner candlelight . . .'

We discussed the Japanese language and the difficulties which

The 7th HIRONO

Hirono—the 7th hole

face travellers to all foreign lands. Someone commented on illogical English with the example 'Wouldn't you like a drink?' We always say 'yes', but that means 'Yes, I wouldn't like a drink!' Lest he should be considered impolite, the speaker hurriedly mentioned the many golfing terms which have an amusing twist in Japanese. Instead of saying 'If we play golf to-morrow', in Japan one would say 'If to-morrow golfs,' and instead of reminding your partner 'It's my honour', you say 'I honour of to'. The prefix 'O' was explained to me in detail. It means 'honourable', but really should only be used when the matter under discussion is personal. I submitted 'In Japan, when you slice your ball into sand you are not merely in a bunker, you are in an honourable hazard.' The party were good enough to laugh, agreeing that few things in life are more personal than bunkers.

Brief explorations into the Japanese language taught me there are ways not merely of describing, or explaining. In Japan, one can also indicate a state of mind. This is called *kimochi*, and *kimochi*, of course, is invaluable in love-making and golf. I believe Japanese to be the best language for golf, and it is a pity that English words have been so quickly brought into the game, in Japan. It makes Britons proud, and for visitors it is very convenient, but, let's face it, with a language like Japanese available it is nonsensical to use English for a game in which the state of mind is so important.

The Japanese have a word *kami*, which means 'over, above, a leader'. This could apply to a golfer, but he must be very special, like Harry Vardon, or maybe Bobby Jones.

I have the impression that the Japanese are keeping *kami* on ice, and one day they may use it when referring to Chen Chin Po, a leading golf professional from Nationalist China. Since he took up domicile in Tokyo he has quickly become one of the most popular men in Japan. He is kindly, unassuming, has a slow Sam Snead swing, which has served him well in international competitions, and, additionally, he has built up a fine reputation as an instructor on T.V., and in the flesh at one of the top Tokyo clubs. Although his home was originally in Taiwan, Chen Chin Po now lives in the capital with a Japanese wife and children. He is an outstanding example of the foreigner who can gain not only complete acceptance, but can rise above colleagues who are Japanese born. This is indicative of the new democratic Japan.

Acceptance of people and life goes deep down into the Japanese mentality. The Golf Widow and I found this to be one of the most charming characteristics. Harmony before logic is pure Buddhism and I was constantly finding myself relating this to golf. The Japanese player appears to regard a golf shot with a certain Buddhist detachment and serenity before advancing to the ball and then becoming intensely pait of the operation of striking. This sounds like the right way, yet we saw some extraordinary spectacles, especially at the driving ranges. But good Japanese golfers seem especially good.

The professional instructors go to tremendous pains to 'put over' their tuition. The learner's attitude is also right. In Japan, the golf pupil accepts unquestioningly what the master says and tries hard to obey. When he is told to keep his head down he does. He never exercises·a prerogative to accept, or disregard, what he is told. Once the pupil has decided to take a course of lessons, his submission to the pro is complete. Sometimes this relationship endures away from golf, and that may by why, even although nearly all professional golfers in Japan have risen from the caddie ranks, they are treated with great respect, despite the class distinction which denies them the use of the clubhouse.

Having played and written of Hirono, lingering over other clubs would be anti-climax. We visited many and discussed more, including those at Kawana which, under surprising circumstances, were created by Baron Okura, who died in 1963.

Like our good friend Mr Takahata, Kischichiro Okura spent years in England. He is the other Japanese responsible for making fine golf courses. But there ends the similarity between these two splendid seniors. Takahata's golf course was created by dedicated intention; the Baron's were made almost by accident.

The circumstances are best explained in the Baron's own words. Among the papers he left was the following:

'The dream of my youth was to own a meadow. I had an eye on the neighbourhood of Ito (in Sagami bay, 50 miles west of Tokyo) for this purpose. I talked it over with the leading residents of the area and finally settled on a stretch of waste land beyond the fishing village of Kawana. Then I started buying territory and when we reached the stage of levelling, a man in charge said the ground composition was predominantly lava ... About a year later I returned on receiving a report that they had finished smoothing. What greeted my eyes was a long extension of green. I got quite a shock and summoned the man in charge, who calmly declared 'The land was unsuitable for a meadow, so I let myself go and made a golf course!" '

That was the beginning, I am assured, of the picturesque links and golfing centre of Kawana. First, the Oshima course was opened in 1928; then C. H. Alison, in Japan to work on other courses, designed a course near to Oshima which Baron Okura named 'Fuji', because golfers have a fine view of the famous mountain. This second links was completed in 1936, and the standard of the two courses was good enough for the 1962 Eisenhower Cup matches. Equidistant from the two championship courses, in fact adjoining them, there is a palatial Gleneagles-style hotel. The whole set-up is lush, picturesque golf, particularly for the affluent, who may well be humbled by the great mountain, towering up behind.

Mount Fuji is the greatest of Japan's twenty national parks, also it is the most beautiful volcano in the world. Each year more than 100,000 Japanese climb the mountain and nearly as many folk play golf on the Kawana links. The villages on Fuji were once owned by feudal overlords. Down below, people apprehensive of battle glanced up at the mountain strongholds and said 'Watch for women leaving and muskets entering.'

Now, they keep their eye on the ball.

Having completed our provincial calls, the Golf Widow and I entrained for Tokyo. The prospect of another sojourn in a city did not enthral. We are country or seaside birds and we had left our hearts at Hirono.

Italian writer Fosco Maraini said of Tokyo: 'Here there meet and mingle the twenty-six civilisations of Toynbee, the eighteen religions of Turchi, von Eicksted's thirty-eight races and sub-races of mankind, the fifty-six ways of making love of the Kama-Sutra, the seventy styles of cooking, the 6 perfumes, the 82 smells, the 120,000 stinks, the twelve dozen kinds of dirt, the seven wonders, the thousand lights, the 2,000 tongues, the thirty-four vices . . .' Including, no doubt, golf which is being denied Tokyo's hungry citizens mainly because of land scarcity.

Sitting alongside us in the train, a charming Japanese professor from the Kyoto University engaged us in conversation. Japanese people chat freely, and when they quickly ask where

FUJI from HAKONE VALLEY

Mount Fuji is the greatest of Japan's twenty national parks

you are going it is not rudeness. In fact, the contrary, for personal questions are a polite way of showing interest.

I told the professor the object of our visit, and asked if he played.

'No,' he said, 'I don't play. In Japan we have so little land to spare. *Golf is against my principles of life.*'

CHAPTER TWELVE

Dindo and Wack Wack

EVERYTHING HAPPENS TO US. The day we arrived in the Philippines, evening newspapers announced that the temperature had reached 99.4°.

Through a brisk shower of perspiration, the Golf Widow read: 'Manilans are sweltering in the sun—the hottest day for twenty years. It is the highest temperature in the city since 5th June, 1946, when the mercury reached 99.6°F. Experts at the weather bureau fear that the coming days may be hotter'.

The flight from Tokyo had been 'slightly turbulent' and that was because 'traffic density' had necessitated flying at 30,000 feet, instead of 35,000 feet. The East is full of surprises and if the stratosphere can be crowded nothing is impossible.

In Bangkok the thermometer had fluttered around a damp 100° so I reckoned we could manage Manila. In any case, prior to thrashing around the golf courses there was leisurely home-work to be done and that would not take so' much energy. You cannot arrive in an important country like the Philippines—which for me had so far been only a name on a Del Monte Pineapple label—to write about the golf, without assimilating some back-ground. To do this I posed questions (so that the Golf Widow could get down the answers) to our Manila hostess, the know-ledgeable Rosalie, who is the wife of Neil Anderson, a top amateur golfer. Neil is employed by Warner Barnes, the great Asian merchants who started golf in the Philippines with a course laid out for the use of their staff at the close of the 19th century.

I should not have said that previously the Philippines to me meant only pineapples because I also knew of Ben Arda. I had seen the Shell 'Wonderful World of Golf' film in which the Filipino had trounced Dow Finsterwald by three strokes, to win £2,500, the biggest cash prize ever offered in the Philippines. Also, I knew of Luis Silverio, the 'Joe Carr of the Philippines',

Luis Silverio
— Philippines

who had beaten Casper, Littler, Thomson and dozens of other professionals in the Philippines Open Championship at Wack Wack. This young man is a great character, in fact, one could say he is a national hero whose memory may well be perpetuated by a statue in the city centre. Once, at a charity golf tournament, players who had better net scores were given gold tie pins inscribed 'I beat Luis Silverio!'

We intended to meet these giants if possible, but for the background to golf in the Philippines the most important man for me was that incorrigible ball of golfing fire whom everyone in the Far East knows as 'Dindo' Gonzalez. We had exchanged breezy letters and I had gathered that Dindo knows all about golf in these parts of the world.

Accepted throughout the China Seas as 'Mr Golf', 'Dindo' Gonzalez is first and foremost a colourful personality. Secondly, he is a great administrator. We played together at Wack Wack and he demonstrated that he is also a very fine golfer. As President of the Philippines Amateur Golf Association he is more powerful than anyone in the western world would guess, if they were basing their assessment on the golf presidents they have known in other countries. P.A.G.A. in the Philippines is the R. and A., the P.G.A. and every other golf governing body rolled into one. The Phillipines Amateur Golf Association makes the rules, organises national and international tournaments, controls professionals, and sells equipment. So far as golf in the Philippines is concerned, P.A.G.A. rules the roost, Dindo rules P.A.G.A., the whole affair works splendidly, and everybody is very happy. With the utmost delicacy, I must explain why.

Serious golf started in the Philippines just after the First World War, but in those days (and even today) the game was only for the rich. P.A.G.A. is now in the process of bringing golf to the masses, and the first positive step in this direction was taken when, acting from strength as an official body, P.A.G.A urged the government to exempt golf equipment from taxation. This has kept the prices of golf clubs and balls relatively low. As soon as the new municipal courses are ready everyone can have a go.

To-day there are more than fifty golf courses in the Philippines, and at least 30,000 golfers, a large percentage of whom are P.A.G.A. members. As in the United States, when a golf addict was the President, the game is increasing in popularity because President Ferdinand E. Marcos is a regular performer who loves the game. He is on record as saying to his cabinet: 'Municipal golf courses are needed. I must do this for the people'.

The costs of promoting the Philippines Open, the oldest and the first fixture on the Far East circuit, have always been borne by the Wack Wack Club. It is a matter of at least £10,000 and for the 1966 event the Club hesitated to carry the burden. Expenses and wages had increased . . . Then it became known that President Marcos would be disappointed if the club pulled out. So the cash was found and the prizes were bigger than ever.

In the palace grounds, the President has reactivated a small golf course which a non-golfing predecessor had bulldozed out of existence. These high-level aspects of Philippines golf are slipped into the narrative to show that now the Golf Widow and I were firmly entrenched in golf's political belt. Before long these pages will be studded with the names of prime ministers, ambassadors, diplomats, and even kings. Golf makes brothers of us all and in the Far East the game could well become the way to achieve peaceful co-existence.

In the meantime, back to Dindo in the P.A.G.A. offices on the outskirts of Manila.

'The Philippines Republic', said the boss, spreading out a large map, 'consists of 7,000 chartered islands, and every time a volcano erupts we get another'.

He pointed to a small island near the southern tip of the archipelago. 'This is Jolo where the inhabitants grow coconuts, pineapples, avocados, mangoes, oranges, santol, jackfruit, sugar cane and bananas. The people who live there are mostly Mohammedans and the rougher element shoot arrows at each other, having first tourniqued their limbs with vine creepers to prevent bleeding . . .'

Dindo laid out an architect's drawing. 'I have here', he said, 'the plan for the new Jolo golf course'.

Then we were told the story of an Irish Roman Catholic bishop who one day arrived in Dindo's office and announced that he and others wanted golf on their tropical island. The aspect was not specifically mentioned, but Dindo got the impression that the Bishop thought to spread Catholicism this way!

Land had been acquired, but much cash was needed to prepare it, and build a clubhouse. 'I shall go to America and appeal to rich friends to help the poor Muslims on this forgotten island', said the Bishop.

A Muslim Congressman and a Chinese landowner from Jolo, also potential golfers, arrived at the P.A.G.A. offices a month later. Then Dindo visited Jolo (a trip which took three hours in a small aircraft) and the work of laying out the golf course started. Prospects are exciting. Take, for example, the specially requested giant 6th hole. It is played from a high tee and stretches down 620 yards of fairway!

Jolo is only to be found on a very large scale map, so it may be useful for you to know that the island is in the Mindanao group. A Muslim and a Chinese, aided and abetted by an Irish bishop, producing golf for simple Mohammedan people living among pineapple groves on an island on the southern tip of the

Philippines . . . What further evidence is necessary that golf is on the march?

For more than three hundred years the Philippines were ruled from Spain. Although in those days the Miguel brothers and Ramon Sota were not there to win golf tournaments, other Spaniards left their mark in many ways. But for the Spanish occupation, for example, there would never have been the crumbling city walls as hazards on the 17th hole at Muni, which is really the Manila Municipal course in the heart of the city. We looked it over and found much new talent taking the first tentative steps in our difficult game. Most Manila golfers start at Muni because it is cheap and easily accessible from city businesses. The course is short and tight, but serves a useful purpose.

After the Spanish-American war, the United States took over Cuba and the Philippines, and the latter was an American Colony until the Japanese came in December, 1941. Few cities have been bombed and fought over more than Manila and Dindo told stories of indomitable golfers throwing themselves into bunkers as low-flying Japanese strafers came down on the Wack Wack course.

What troubles they endure, these brave hackers! Up country, at the Zamboanga club a player who overshoots the 6th green has a good chance of having his leg snapped off by a crocodile! This course was laid out in 1911 under the direction of General John J. Pershing, who should have known that golfers hate to have their legs snapped off.

Shortly before our visit, the fine Capitol Hills golf club was devastated by a tornado. The Club President told me that at the time putting was very difficult! One of the 9 holes courses at Capitol Hills has electric light facilities for after-dark golf and on this course alone the tornado damage entailed great sacrifices from addicts who prefer the cool of nocturnal golf.

More than any race I know the Filipinos have an obsession for education. Every parent has this as a first consideration for the children, and in the P.A.G.A. offices we saw a fine trophy for which the youngsters play. It was presented by the American golf architect, Robert Trent Jones, and is competed for on an inter-schools basis. The 1966 holder of the cup is a young Goliath named Edmundo Unson, Jr., to whom I unwisely offered by hand in greeting. When the crushed bones were healed I had a wonderful game of golf with his father and you will learn of that later.

Edmundo Unson, Jr., is by far the most promising young golfer whom we met on this tour. His father, realising his son's potential, wrote to Arnold Palmer for advice. Palmer, who had seen the boy's swing, agreed that he was an 'outstanding natural' (he hits the ball further than Jack Nicklaus) and suggested that young Edmundo should immediately be put into the capable hands of Byron Nelson. And if that is not a great compliment to Mr Nelson I don't know what is.

Dindo's office at P.A.G.A. is like Aladdin's cave with trophies. We inspected the pure gold Putra Cup which was presented by the Tunku Abdul Rahman of Malaysia to be competed for by the South-East Asia countries to 'preserve peace through golf'. The number of times I heard people say that this is more sensible than spending money on polaris submarines was most gratifying.

In addition to trophies and tons of golf equipment, Dindo's emporium contains the answer to any question you may ask regarding golf in the Philippines. I enquired about Luis Silverio.

'Luis is twenty-eight years old, 5′ 6″ tall, and weighs 130 lbs. He hits a long ball using a heavy driver with an 'E. Zero' shaft. He is Amateur Champion of the Philippines and manages a golf club factory . . .' I learned about the golfer's health, habits, home life, and of the fine Marapara golf course which Silverio had laid out near the Marapara Mountains at Bacolod City.

This man Dindo is astonishing. He has an encyclopaedic brain, lives well, works tremendously hard (often without recompense) and deserves the kind of fourteen-servant luxury he enjoys in his beautiful Manila home. He has three sons, a daughter, and a brother who is the Philippines Ambassador in Madrid.

In addition to being the head of golf in the Republic, Dindo Gonzalez is the Chairman of a large advertising agency, a radio executive, and a competent journalist with a weekly column in the *Manila Times* which is generally regarded as a funnel through which blows all the news and golfing chit-chat of South-East Asia. In the United States, Dindo would have been a Senator, but that would not have suited him, because although he is very American, his background is pure Spanish and he probably accepts his native proverb that it is 'Better to be head of a mouse than tail of a lion'.

Celestino Tugot
—— PHILIPPINES

He took me to play a round of golf at Wack Wack.

No golf club in the Far East is better known or has done more for golf as an international spectacle. There are two fine courses and the 'East' is championship class according to any standards. The lay-out is on pleasantly wooded, rolling land, convenient to the heart of Manila.

The Wack Wack East course record is a five under par 67, held by Celestino Tugot, who has continued to win cash prizes after becoming a grandfather. At the time of writing Tugot is the resident professional at the Del Monte (pineapple) club, which has one of the most picturesque little courses in the Philippines with the advantage of no charges, since the club exists purely for Del Monte personnel and their guests.

Gene Sarazen once played a terrific match at Wack Wack and was narrowly beaten by the local golfer, Larry Montes. 'Whenever anyone breaks par on this thing', said Sarazen, 'please let me know'. It seldom happens. At the top of his form the Australian Norman von Nida won the Philippines Open with 293 for 72 holes. Which highlights Luis Silverio's 287 in 1966.

Wack Wack has seen the most astonishing sights, not the least being Eric Brown the Scot, looking like an Arab, draped with a towel to keep off the sun; maybe it was also to hide his shame at missing an eleven inch putt for a big cash prize. In the same tournament, when Ben Arda had a putt hovering on the brink, a wild Filipino broke through the ropes and did a voodoo dance on the green. The ball didn't drop.

Despite performing my usual 'ball in the pond' act at the end, I enjoyed my game with Dindo. President Marcos, who manages to slip in two or three rounds a week, was playing just ahead of us, very competently I thought. Then, with the Golf Widow, we sat on the club verandah and enjoyed beakers of iced coconut milk from palms casting their shadows on the first tee.

I would say that Wack Wack is pricey, but it is tremendously popular and although this was a working day, happy Filipinos were there in droves. I met the Club President (they don't have a Captain) and learnt about the club administration. Strangely, in addition to the normal committees, there is also a legal section 'to take care of eventualities' if anyone gets hit with a golf ball!

Dindo showed us a thing of great beauty which must be unique in golf. The championship course has been built in miniature over an area of perhaps an acre and a half. Trees, lakes, hazards, slopes . . . They are all there and a golfer can play the course leisurely with his putter.

One of the things that fascinated me about Wack Wack was the name. Apparently there was much deliberation on this point, and all agreed that the label must be original for such an outstandingly fine club. The first President was responsible and the circumstances were unusual. Trying out the new course, he had teed up his ball when two fierce crows descended. One grabbed the ball and flew off. The other cawed indignantly wack- wack-wack . . . So that became the club name and the emblem is two crows and a golf ball.

As one would expect, the locker-rooms at Wack Wack are *grande luxe*. Stewards hover around, packing bags, offering drinks, talcum powder, hot baths and solace. Also, there is a competent staff of masseurs. In the United States I have em-

Everything at Wack Wack is grande luxe

ployed this kind of service. A massage is an agreeable finale to a tiring round, and at Wack Wack Dindo probably thought that I needed reviving.

'It's all arranged', he said. 'Have your shower then Garcia will take you to the massage room'.

It was, in fact, all arranged. Four men worked on me, a masseur for each leg, one for my chest and tummy, and the director of operations who stood behind my head making sooth-ing strokes on my neck and shoulders. I was oiled, cooled off with alcohol, then sprinkled with fragrant talc from a large canister which more than ever made me feel like a lump of well-kneaded dough ready for the oven.

Garcia dressed me. Then I went to appease the Golf Widow who had been kicking her heels for about an hour on the verandah, the only lady among a crowd of Filipinos.

CHAPTER THIRTEEN

Philippines Fly-Around

IN THE WHOLE WORLD I don't suppose any other golf club could name each of eighteen holes after a different species of tree growing on the course. That is what they have been able to do at the Manila Golf and Country Club and for the sake of horticulturists here is a the list starting from the first hole: Narra, Acacia, Chico, Dao, Pili, Caballero, Santol, Banana, Avocado, Guava, Lauan, Kakawate, Nanka, Ipil, Tamarind, Agoho, Dapdap, Mango. The shortest hole is Chico—the 3rd, and the longest is Mango—the 18th.

Here is a fine golf course, short by championship standards, but cut out of timbered country on gently undulating land, and bunkered with imagination and the spice of devilry that only a Scottish architect could devise. In a four day tournament with a hundred golfers, never more than two broke par on any day. Each year, by arrangement with P.A.G.A., the Amateur Championship was held here. The meeting suited the setting, just as Wack Wack is more fitting for the senior pro-tournaments.

The Manila Club has a homely, family atmosphere (no masseurs here) with plenty of tradition, being one of the oldest golf clubs in the Philippines.

When Gary Player tackled the course in an exhibition with Palmer, he wiped his brow with the back of his hand and said 'One of the best tracks I know'. A little prejudiced maybe, because he had just broken the course record with a 65, nevertheless, he merely repeated what has been said many times.

A man who never ceases singing its praises is Ben Arda, and this is also to be expected since Ben was the Manila Club professional. We were disappointed not to see him; he was absent playing in the Taipei Open. In fact during that same afternoon he had holed-in-one at the 17th at the Taiwan Country Club at Tamsui, a fact that caused great jubilation among folk at the club. These included his brothers Margarita and Vicente, with whom I had a chat about Ben. They kept an eye on things and gave lessons when big brother was away. On return, we learnt that the Ardas have now left the club. Pity.

Filipinos marry young and Ben Arda had a wife when he was seventeen and a grandchild before he was thirty-five. His parents had twelve children; Ben had five. Like his friend, Celestino Tugot, who is also a grand-dad, Ben can compete in any company, and make good money on the American circuit which is rather more than our British home products have done since the days of Harry Vardon.

Although the Manila Club goes back to 1901, the course was not then located at Makati. The present lay-out was designed by Jim Black, a Scottish Canadian, and all of this I learnt during much talk with Wallace McGregor Davis, a bit of old Aberdeen, who seems to have administrative control in a kindly way. A member said that Wally rules with a 'benevolent rod of iron' and mentioned certain 'Wally foibles' on the course, like 'nests of bunkers', and twelve mango trees where for years there have only been five. . . . Allegedly, Wally gnashes his teeth every time par is broken. Nevertheless, he has good ideas. On the first tee, for example, he has instigated a changeable board to inform players about the greens which are 'under dresssing', 'being aerated', or 'on top shelf'.

Maybe Wally does rule with a rod of iron, but all this spells dedication, and that is how good golf is made.

There are about thirty British members at the Manila Club, and possibly twice as many made up from a dozen or so other European countries, but most members are first generation golfers, born and bred in the Philippines.

There are one or two purely American Services golf clubs in the Republic; the Clark course is the best and this is to be expected since they spent £20,000 on the underground watering system. Then there is the John Hay Air Base Golf Club, with the enviable reputation as 'one of the finest recreation centres under the American flag'. Also, there are one or two golf clubs for Filipino officers, like the Philippines Navy Compound. Each of these is detailed in a splendid report, lovingly prepared and given to me by Mr Z. M. Tabaniag of the great Caltex Oil Company. I have a shrewd idea that Mr Tabaniag is first and foremost a golfer, although he protests that he is really an oil man. His report is prefaced: 'Golf is sweeping the Philippines. . . . Golfing minds refuse to buckle under the handicaps of difficult terrain, or clime, or just plain impecuniosity. . . . You can feel the feverish zeal. Even sand dunes, or parched, turfless terrain cannot faze staunch hearts. . . .'

There were about forty courses in play when we were in the Philippines and to have visited them all would have been an island hopping adventure taking much too long. We were therefore obliged merely to dip in, here and there, as our counsellors recommended.

About four hundred miles south of Manila, on one of the smaller islands, there is the Cebu Golf Club. In Manila, friends said: 'You must go to Cebu. That is where Ben Arda and Celestino Tugot started as caddies'. I suppose things must be kept in proportion, and it is unlikely that these names will mean much to 99 out of 100 readers, but Ben and Celestino are national idols in the Philippines. Well, they started their golf at Cebu, and here we found much of interest including maybe the most difficult golf hole in the Far East.

The 14th at Cebu is called Hibok Hibok and is generally accepted as a sadist's creation. The yardage is only 362, but a great ravine in front of the tee traps your drive if it falls short of 200 yards, so if this is inevitable you might as well move on to the next hole. If you carry the ravine there are other novelties . . . . A medal should be struck and presented on the green to those who are there in two shots. Like many golf clubs in the Philippines, Cebu had early difficulties. Although a start was made in 1912 (it is one of the oldest) there have been gaps. But all that is in the past. Prosperity is now in view and if only they could do something about the 14th. . . .

Many of the courses in the Philippines are similar in character. Excepting for those on high land, the greens are usually 'hard' grass—Bermuda or korai; invariably there are water problems, and the trees are usually acacia and mango. So we ferreted out the unusual, like Cagayan de Oro. Here, in the southerly Mindanao region (not so far from Jolo), they have a problem which we had never met before. At the 8th and 9th hole an aircraft runway crosses the fairways! Never mind, Dr Perfecto Casino, the club president, and his enthusiastic board accept the interruptions with admirable philosophy.

A Mr Ah Fat Yu New has put up a concrete slab at the 4th

hole to commemorate a triumphant hole-in-one on May 15th, 1953, and this evidence of justifiable pride shows how important these things have become in the Far East.

We found the Filipinos a happy, colourful people, but Dindo Gonzalez told us of the inhabitants of Laoag who are also thrifty. In fact, they are called 'Philippines Scotsmen', and I hope they are proud of the title. At any rate they are plucky, for they have hacked out nine respectable golf holes from the unsympathetic heart of 'water buffalo country'. Strangely enough, so many courses are being laid out in places like this that the unattractive but docile water buffalo may well become extinct.

New courses are springing up almost overnight, particularly on the large northerly island of Luzon, and I hope there will never be a golf recession through over-production. For example, it will be a pity if the new course at Angeles City does not prosper. It is called the Paradise Golf Club and the prime mover is the governor of Pampanga, who has given over a stretch of his estate for the worthy purpose.

Perhaps the most ambitious of the new clubs is the Apo Golf Club at Davao; at the time of writing this is the most southerly 18 holes in play. Here is an unusually fine terrain cleared from a coconut plantation—in fact the club gets substantial revenue from that source—and has all the water required. Which is more than can be said of Baguio, where the 'greens' are 'browns', but so beautifully kept that 'we wouldn't have it otherwise', said a member with commendable defiance.

I have always admired the tremendous loyalty a golfer has for his terrain. To his clubmates he will curse and swear about everything from workmen to wormcasts. But let any outsider mumble one word of criticism and he immediately grasps his wedge to strike a blow in defence of his course. Something like this will happen when my friend Dindo Gonzalez (whose Latin paddy must be something terrible to see) reads that I don't consider Wack Wack to be the best course in the Philippines.

Dindo is a Wack Wack man and will fight to the death anyone who does not agree that W.W. is the finest. Now, I have to say that I prefer the Valley course. So does Dindo's friend, Edmundo Unson. In fact, he it was who took me there and gave me a 4 and 3 thrashing as part of the bargain.

The Valley Golf and Country Club is at Antipolo, about

fifteen miles from Manila. Like most of the best golf in the Far East it was carefully planned on a sound, financial, real estate basis. It did not arrive by accident, as one imagines say Westward Ho! did, or like many of the Scottish courses that started in the hoary past on pieces of unwanted land, where men could 'play a few holes' for peaceful recreation.

The brochure states; 'Valley Golf and Country Club represents the epitome of the recent development of Philippines golf. It has demonstrated what money, wisely invested, can do'.

The project started with 200 members, who invested £1,000 each for proprietary rights—they were each to have an adjoining plot of land on which to build a villa. This initial £200,000 proved insufficient, so there was a second issue of 200 shares, but by now the price was up to £2,000 each. That added another £400,000. Then, because the public was getting interested (and more cash was needed), it was decided to launch a third issue of 400 at £1,700, but this time the holders did not get plots of land—making another £680,000. At the time of writing £1,280,000 had gone into making the club and this sort of thing rather frightens me. As with most humble Britons, my golf has been pleasant, rather cheese-paring stuff, wherein the purchase of a new gang-mower has taken at least three committee meetings and long harangues with the bank.

With all the cash the Valley had, given also some common sense, it was certain that they would produce a crackerjack golf course. In my opinion it is terrific and second only to Hirono, in Japan, of all we inspected.

The clubhouse is a most revolutionary work of functional art designed by Gabriel Formoso, who lives nearby. Revolutionary, because it is fashioned in the shape of the tee on which you balance your golf ball, and as part of the ensemble, poised in the right place, there is a giant golf ball (with the correct number of dimples) holding 50,000 gallons of water. Seen from the 4th tee, about half a mile away, this vast ingenious creation is breath-taking and, strangely enough, quite beautiful. The clubhouse is also functional and all the curves and sloping walls have been carefully designed to catch every small breeze to keep the verandahs pleasantly cool. Indoors there is, of course, air-conditioning throughout.

The land, which the Valley Golf Club company bought in 1959, had been a dairy farm owned by Mr Hardie, a man of Scottish ancestry. Along with his wife, he was tragically murdered by bandits. The trustees first offered the land to the Wack Wack Club, who have never stopped regretting their refusal to purchase because golf fits into this particular countryside like a well-chosen jewel in an emperor's crown.

The course is about 7,000 yards, and was originally laid out by 'a Scot named Scott' (that was as accurate as I could get) and further developed by Mr Freddy Smith of Carter's Seed Company. The lay-out combines classical golf holes with the drama of the landscape. There are lakes (man-made and natural) which intervene at six holes in the home 9; lovely trees, and fine greens of Tifton 328 grass brought specially from Texas in growing slabs. Only after great deliberation was this species of grass chosen and the final decision was wise.

When inevitable teething troubles have been overcome, golf at Valley will be comparable with the best, anywhere.

Edmundo Unson, Sr, our host, is on the board of directors of the company and he showed us the plot of land on which he will eventually build a fine house. Also he demonstrated how easy it is to smack a golf ball sweetly, if the mechanism is right. We had an enjoyable game, and when Edmundo had two surprising shanks at the 6th my heart warmed to him. He doesn't know how much he did at that moment to further Anglo-Philippines amity.

The inward 9 holes are described as 'more challenging golf', but the whole course is delightful, particularly if your are hitting a few good shots. In any case, the caddies keep you happy. At a pond hole, my boy told me to play short. I dismally topped and the ball skittered along the ground, finally coming to rest about a foot from the water's edge.

'Only a professional could stop as near as that,' said my caddie.

Picturesque women were weeding some of the greens; they sat in groups of maybe half-a-dozen, working conscientiously but chatting as matrons would at a sewing bee. They wore white conical hats, known as *salakots*, with white scarves to prevent even a flicker of sunshine getting through to their handsome faces. Also, they had umbrellas, one between two, and 1 daresay all these protections are necessary when they have to sit for hours in the scorching sun.

We had a delightful lunch in a dining room that could have

The clubhouse from 4th tee
VALLEY G.C. Philippines ⟶

**The clubhouse at 'Valley' is a revolutionary work
of functional art**

taken a banquet of hundreds. Edmundo introduced me to Mr Marcial Lichauco, who had recently returned from being Ambassador in London. He and his wife were entertaining the Fung Ping-Fans from Hong Kong. Ivy Fung Ping-Fan told me a funny story. She is golf addicted. One day, on discovering she had forgotten to bring golf sockettes to wear with her heavy shoes, she accepted a spare pair produced by a strange man. Ivy said they were the grubbiest, holiest, old socks she had ever seen, but golfers don't care so she wore them.

'Do you know,' said Ivy, 'in the first nine holes, I had five bogeys and a birdie! Those socks worked wonders, but of course I had to return them. That was two months ago and *I haven't had a bogey since!*'

CHAPTER FOURTEEN

Song of Singapore

WE HAD BEGUN to regard green grass as something rare and precious. Then we reached Singapore.

Golf in most parts of India, Thailand, Hong Kong, Japan, Philippines . . . requires seeds or sods from Bermuda, Egypt, Texas, Uganda, and goodness knows where. Then, to make the stuff grow without water, men with green fingers must be found. It is wizard's work.

Rich clubs like Fanling, Willingdon, Wack Wack and Royal Bangkok usually suceed in producing very fair putting surfaces at about £1,000 per green per annum. In Singapore it is quite different.

We had read all about humidity, so the sight of hundreds of emerald acres should not have been such a shock. But it was. Then I had a pleasant sensation of relief because I knew that I would be spared the heart-rending Secretary stories of bad grass and impossible golfing conditions.

The Bukit course at the Island Club is green and lush. Hills slope down to a beautiful lake (which is really a reservoir made years ago by a man named McRitchie), and a dense jungle seals off one side. On the course there are 3,021 trees. The Secretary had them counted, and they include casuarinas, tambusus and rain trees. Which brings me to the downpour I watched from our apartment at Air House.

If you can imagine anything nicer than a full view of a lovely green golf course from your bed, I can't.

After a long flight, we had arrived late on a starlit tropical night. We slept wonderfully, then, very early, our first daylight view was of a rolling fairway. I drank it in, then yelled across to my wife to sit up in bed and view a brace of golfers, with caddies, trudging through the dawn dew.

It must have been darkish when they drove off. This was the

2nd fairway, and when I later asked about the golfers our hostess said: 'Yes, that would be Joe Cashim and his friend. They start every day before night finishes.'

By 6.30 a.m. there are always between thirty and forty cars outside the Bukit clubhouse. This is the best time for Singapore golf; the grass is cool, and baby monkeys playing on the fairways are shepherded by their mothers into the safety of the jungle. As the day begins, water buffaloes, rats, squirrels, shrews, bats, and even flying foxes with four-feet wing span, move deeper into the jungle alongside the 14th fairway. Early golfers once found a six-foot cobra, and in the men's bar there is the stuffed head of a magnificent boar, shot on the 11th green, July 10, 1950.

Birds on the Singapore courses include the yellow-tipped bulbul, the golden oriole, and kingfishers blue as the sky. Also, there are tame lizards (*chichak*), and forty species of not so tame snakes. On no golf course in the world does flora and fauna flourish as in Singapore.

I watched the golfers, and quite suddenly the rose pink dawn became leaden grey and before my sleepy brain had registered the change, the whole firmament burst in a deluge of rain. Joe Cashim and his buddy, no doubt accustomed to this sort of thing, vanished, and within minutes the fairway was awash.

These violent downpours are known locally as *sumatras*. They must be experienced to be thoroughly believed and the only good thing about them is that they seldom last for more than minutes. Then the land drains, hot sunshine makes the landscape steamy, and the sky looks so innocent that you think you've imagined the whole affair.

Immediately prior to heavy rain, there is usually lightning followed by crackling stage-effect thunder. Golfers don't hang about under these conditions, although we learnt of a Japanese lawyer who had been fatally struck 'right at the top of his back-swing', according to his caddie.

The weather does not often interfere with golf in Singapore. Every season is the same and of this fact we were reminded each morning as we took breakfast on the verandah at Air House. In view, there was a huge tree which is always in bud on the uppermost branches, heavily foliaged lower down, and near the ground it sheds brown leaves. Poor thing. It doesn't know whether it is going or coming. How could it?—in a mid-day temperature

'THE · RELUCTANT MODEL'

which throughout the year never varies more than three degrees.

Singapore Island is about the size of the Isle of Wight, roughly the same shape, but closer to Malaya than Cowes is to the mainland of Hampshire. There are eight golf clubs on the island, plus the Island Country Club which has three eighteen holes courses, named Bukit, Island and Sime. These are referred to as 'locations'.

In the old days, the Royal Singapore Golf Club had Bukit Timah (Tin Hill) and Sime (laid out by James Braid); membership was exclusively British. The Island Club was cosmopolitan. Now, the courses all come under the banner 'The Singapore Island Country Club', and membership (when available) does not depend on race or creed.

These ancient British institutions have fascinating histories. When Mr Justice Goldney drove off the first official golf ball in

H

Singapore, the course was on the old race track. The year was 1891, and the distinguished gentleman wore bright green knickerbockers, a stiff collar, white tie, orthodox red jacket, and a bowler hat. This is the kind of magnificent intelligence one can acquire from the old records.

When the cosmopolitan Island Club got going, the members were Filipinos, Indonesians, Indians, Pakistanis, Singalese, Americans, Canadians, Teochews, Hokkiens, Hainanese, Malaysians, Arabs, Armenians, Taoists, and assorted Europeans. As one would expect, the club was overcrowded. By 1963, the time had come for the Island Club and Royal Singapore to unite. So the 'Singapore Island Country Club' was re-constituted to administer the three courses, and the 4,000 members can now play their choice.

The symbol of the Island Country Club is a white sea eagle, a handsome bird seen in these parts and chosen by a distinguished ornithologist who was President of the new administration.

We shall return to the Island Club, but first one should review the other golf courses in Singapore.

Ever since the island was a British garrison, Army, Navy, and particularly the Royal Air Force personnel have satisfied their individual golfing hungers. For example, there are three R.A.F. golf clubs and these are sprinkled more or less around the coast adjoining the air bases.

Seleter—9 holes; with well cared for greens.

Tengah—9 holes; to the west of the island.

Changi—9 holes; an 'around-the-houses' course.

Subscriptions are according to rank: squadron leaders and above pay 12s 6d a month.

The Warren Golf Club (mostly Army) had some roughish holes of rather 'undisciplined' golf when we were there and a hearty hook puts you among the gin slings on the patio. This club (for some involved reason) is the only one on the Island that does not belong to the Singapore Golf Association.

A comparatively new course, mainly for serving personnel, is at the Sembawang Naval Base. The track has been named 'H.M.S. Terror'.

Keppel is a charming 9 holes, administered by the harbour board and is situated on the southern seaboard of the island.

In all, at the time of writing, there are 117 holes of golf on the island of Singapore, and as Lee Kuan Yew, the golfing Prime Minister, has said with pride: 'In no city in south-east Asia are there as many courses.' Let it be noted that he followed this remark with 'a legacy of British colonialism. . . .'

The Prime Minister, a good 12 handicap player, wants to give a new municipal course to his people; one has already been prospected and a start will certainly be made before this book is in print.

The Prime Minister of Singapore went to Cambridge University. His handicap was 12 when we were there, but erosion was in progress. He did a hole-in-one at the 8th at Cameron Highlands, an up-country course in Malaysia, and his Finance Minister, Mr Goh Ken Swee, quickly followed suit at the same hole on the same golf course.

I missed my game with the Prime Minister and that was the only thing that went wrong during our visit to Singapore. Our flight plan had been unavoidably changed. In consequence, we lost a day which unfortunately included the afternoon when Mr Lee Kuan Yew had kindly agreed to play with me. Later, we read in the newspapers that Premier Harold Wilson made amends for my absence by giving the Singapore Prime Minister a knock on the Ellesborough course when he visited England for defence talks. But it wasn't the same.

With permission, I quote Mr Lee Kuan Yew on his favourite subject:

'There was a time when golf was considered a decadent pastime of the wealthy and the idle. Newly independent countries eager for industrial advance are not supposed to have much time for decadent sport. Attitudes are slowly changing as more and more executives in commerce, industry and administration in newly independent countries discover that golf is a valuable reprieve from the pressures of smoky committee rooms which appear to be the inevitable lot of all those who have to decide the policy of corporations or of governments.'

My game with the Prime Minister was to have been played at the Bukit club, and for kindly engineering the arrangement I am indebted to Cyril Horne and this was not the only thing he did for us.

Cyril, twin brother of Ryder Club player, Reg Horne, was the professional at Littlestone in Kent until 1961 when he was appointed to Singapore. Since then he has prospered. He has kingfishers in his garden and a villa containing precious furniture, ming vases, objet d'arts, and so many nice things bought on his travels that one wonders whether Cyril is a golf professional or an antique dealer! Actually, this most enterprising maestro works his head off at the game and is spreading golf's gospel far and wide.

Horne's business (I suppose one can call it that) in Singapore is terriffic. He has a three-tiered floodlit driving range which does a roaring trade at 2s 6d for 50 balls, totalling about 7,000 balls on a good day. His list of past and present pupils reads like Debrett, the United Nations, and a Who's Who of South-East Asia. He showed me his appointment book and at random I spotted:

Lee Kuan Yew, Prime Minister of Singapore; Deputy Prime Minister Dr Toh Chin Chye; Minister of Defence Dr Goh Keng Swee; Chief Justice of the High Court Wee Cong Jin (who is also President of the Singapore Golf Association); King of Malaysia; Malaysian Prime Minister Abdul Rahman. . . . To add variety there was Sherpa Tensing of Everest (on a lecture tour), and the name of an Eskimo nurse!

From the shelter of a palm tree, I watched Horne at work. One of his 'group classes' was in progress with six American ladies.

'Not so hard Number 3. Swing slower. You're not a jet. Think of a lovely, smooth crossing in the Queen Mary,' chanted Cyril, and added, 'A little more pivot Number 5. I know we're not as sylphlike as we were but let's kid 'em.'

Then, he finished the class. 'You're all too darn good,' he said. 'How can I get you back again on Thursday if you learn it all to-day?' Everyone laughed and went away happy.

I wonder if the British government realises the ambassador value of chaps like Horne? He is selling the home country every minute of the day and of course that also applies to golf.

Singapore gave this citation: 'Presented to Cyril Horne by Head of State His Excellency Yang di-Pertuan Negara. For services to golf. . . .'

'Cyril of Singapore'
— GOLF PRO EXTRAORDINARY —

Side Issues on the Equator

SIR THOMAS STAMFORD RAFFLES was the first notable Briton to linger in Singapore and he arrived in 1819 to represent the East India Company. One hundred years previously, a Scottish adventurer named Alexander Hamilton settled and on being offered the Isle of Singapore, he diarised: 'It could be of no use to a private person 'tho a proper place for a company to settle in . . . '

Had either of these worthies brought golf clubs the game might have got under way earlier and the present congestion would be even worse. When we were there members booked starting times eight days ahead—and hoped. Casual visitors don't stand a chance, and had I not been 'fitted in' by one of the pillars of the Club, my game with Cyril Horne and Air Marshal Sir Peter Wykeham would never have taken place. The Air Marshal, an old Western Desert comrade, hits a mighty ball, not always straight, but mighty.

We played until night descended without warning, leaving us to walk through the purple night and crackling crickets towards the clubhouse lights half a mile away. Neither dawn nor twilight exist in Singapore, as we know them in Europe. That, I suppose, and the fact that we were playing on the only first-class golf course on the equator made this round memorable.

Of the three Island Country Club courses, Bukit is easily the best. From back tees it stretches to about 6,700 yards. The general impression is of a privately owned golf course in a lovely park. The countryside is wooded and undulating and the distant lake is very Scottish with the 2nd and 3rd holes along the banks. No. 4 is a slogging 498 yards; 5 is short and flanked to the right with swampy jungle; uphill, back towards the clubhouse is the long 6; 7 stretches towards the lake again; 8 calls for 'target' golf; 9 is back to the clubhouse where the custom is to have a quickie. The homeward nine holes are more severe and the 13th

DRIVING
RANGE
BUKIT

(557 yards) is as stiff a par 5 as one will find in these parts.

Peter Thomson took 300 for four rounds in a tournament at Bukit, so if he could do no better than average 75, my assessment is that an additional ten strokes would still keep me respectable.

There is very little run on the ball at the Island Club courses because of moisture and humidity. But the fairways of Kachang grass and the greens of Seragoon are more emerald than any I have seen outside the British Isles, so you can't have it all ways.

The Second World War set the club back. A large area of the main course was used by the Japanese for growing tapioca, an asphalt road was built to a shrine on the summit of the jungle-covered hill overlooking the reservoir, and many of the club trophies and records were lost. But all that is now a story of the dismal past and you would go a long way to see a cheerier midday scene than the terrace at the Bukit club.

Cheerfulness is a characteristic of the Chinese and Malays, but the caddies have an annoying habit of grinning when they give you bad news. As an example, when I pushed a shot perilously close to the edge of the McRitchie reservoir, my caddie positively beamed while telling me that the ball was certainly a goner. It so happened that he was wrong, and I took good care to laugh like hell when telling him that the ball was found.

The Island Club caddies are a race apart, quite different to the gentle souls who carried for me in Japan. I was told they have protection rackets, carry knives and indulge in other practices foreign to the game of golf. Admittedly the Singapore chaps look fierce, but in my opinion they are greatly maligned and no more savage than picture-book pirates. Of course, they all have incandescent breaths, but that is unavoidable if you eat highly-spiced food and many of us would risk that if it could help us to play like the 15 years old youngster we saw who went round the Island location in 70 shots.

Caddies are allowed to play on Monday mornings and the bright ones take advantage of this privilege. Many live in Tambulong kampong near the club. It is customary for native crafts to be segregated in the villages, and not unappropriately, I thought, gravestones are made in the kampong by the Bukit course. Never an easy test. Members who like gentler stuff play Sime.

The Sime course, named after John Sime who actually sited and laid out Bukit, is shorter and easier, but has the same agreeable characteristics of the longer course. The homeward 9 is called 'the goat track' and crosses the older Bukit course. Green 9 is near the clubhouse, and senior members have a tendency to drop in for stengahs which have been known to terminate the round.

Although Sime adjoins Bukit, the Island location is a couple of miles up the road. Here is another splendid golf course with some hilly holes—like 9 and 18, both short, difficult, and (stretching the imagination a trifle) tunnel-like. They climb upwards, between parallel rows of trees. Kel Nagle wrecked a card on 18 by putting his drive out of bounds and taking 7.

We followed a couple of barefooted caddies who were playing hole 18 from one bag containing five clubs. Both put their drives within ten feet of the flag, and one holed out with remarkably little fuss.

We chatted with Jim McInnes, the Australian professional. I asked him why he had come to Singapore, and he answered without hesitation 'For the money', which is fair enough and doubtless true. Like Cyril Horne, he is a fine tutor and his services are greatly sought.

Although shorter and less testing than Bukit, the Island location is a fine golf course with interesting shots for players of all categories. When we were there the greens were even better than those at Bukit and that means they were just about as good as greens can be outside Britain.

Some years ago, the Singapore greens were plagued with white ants who marched in great armies, two feet abreast, leaving a trail of dead grass. As one would expect, there was great consternation. Then a chemist got to work and that was that. Which reminds us that human endeavour can do great things, and not only for golf.

The Singapore Premier told his people that the golf they enjoy is a British legacy. Strangely enough, so is rubber, on which Malaysia's economy is largely based. The very first rubber tree to be planted in these parts came from London's Kew Gardens and it still grows in Singapore with a plaque telling all the world where it came from. To think that off-shoots from this self same tree are hazards on courses all over the island!

We lunched at the Island location clubhouse in the charming upstairs dining room overlooking the swimming pool, the flowers, and the emerald fairways of this attractive golf course.

Here and there, elegant Tamil Indian women walked gracefully, like Rebecca going to the well, but instead of carrying urns on their shoulders they carried baskets of fertiliser which they scattered on the greens by hand as if they were feeding the birds.

Stengahs followed a delicious club luncheon of fried rice and crisp-brown Peking duck. Then came the golf talk, and we learnt of the extraordinary Sultan of Johore.

Across the 800 yards strip of water dividing the Island of Singapore and the mainland, there is the State of Johore which is the source of the Singapore water supply.

The Sultan started golf at the Royal Johore International Club in 1935, but he must have been a tempestuous man. Once, in a fit of pique over some small incident, he commanded his gardeners to work all night planting trees on the greens. Then, within a month, he calmed down and put a hundred men to work on restoring the greens to a condition better than ever!

A man came over to our table and joined the party for what he called a 'sobering coffee' prior to playing golf. He had been to the wedding of a Malay friend and for the benefit of the Golf Widow and me, he described what occurred. Maybe a Malaysian wedding is out of place in this kind of book, but I shall risk it if only to show how golf has slipped into place amid surroundings and influences as different to St Andrews as Singapore orchids are to the homely buttercup.

Friends of the bridegroom had assembled at his parent's house for a gigantic meal, then the groom was escorted to the bride's home where another banquet was taking place. The bride and groom sat in royal state. He was dressed in the traditional wedding ceremonial robes and trappings which his father and grandfather had worn. These included a golden turban, a long scarlet robe with gold embroidery and wide sleeves tight at the wrists, and dozens of bracelets and garlands of orchids.

Later, with his father and mother on either side, the groom led the party down the village street. Throughout, the groom remained solemn, with no flicker of a smile. His male friends larked about, in the traditional manner, trying to get the lad to smile. But he must not do so, for this would foretell of catastrophe, and evil spirits, and an unhappy marriage; they might be denied children, or they would be born with hare lips. . . .

At this point the conversation returned to golf which somehow or other got mixed up with the evil spirits. It appeared that the 14th fairway at Island location is a favourite place for them to linger, and a certain Chinese golfer actually sets off fireworks to frighten evil spirits away, prior to taking his shot!

The strangest things can happen. Cyril Horne told us of when he was making a new golf course in Malacca. Suddenly the ground gave way and he found himself twenty feet down in an old tiger trap! This was in 1964. The Ayer Keroh course in Malacca is open now, just one hundred miles north of Singapore. Hundreds of forest giants had to be uprooted and turf for the greens was brought from Singapore. So were some caged animals for the little zoo by the clubhouse to keep the kiddies amused while their dads are struggling around 7,000 yards of testing golf.

I had previously heard of Ayer Keroh and this can be put down as a Horne triumph despite an unfortunate anti-climax. Poor Cyril, he designed the course, then when it was opened he couldn't get through the dense crowd to tee up for the official drive off by the Prime Minister!

As Horne says, in these parts things seldom turn out as expected. He went to design a course in Indonesia, but what he will do with the tiger promised as part payment, goodness knows.

We left the club for siesta and I was given a paper to read.

Quite astonishingly, but not harmfully, senior politicians in this region make many declarations about golf. I suppose it is natural enough to shout about it when one has made a great new discovery. A senior government official had said: 'On all levels in Singapore, golf is now regarded as a great 20th-century aid to sound commerce, harmonious politics, and international good will.'

Fine! But let us not forget that golf is also a jolly good game.

CHAPTER SIXTEEN

The Fanatics of Kuala Lumpur

GOING ALONG with the idea that Singapore Island is the same size and shape as the Isle of Wight in the South of England, if you skip Devon and Cornwall and travel up the west coast of Malaysia about as far as Liverpool (on the west coast of England) you reach Kuala Lumpur. Being an ancient golfing stronghold and the capital of the country, this was to be our base.

We had fleetingly thought of operating from Penang, but I think it was because the Golf Widow had been reading an Edwardian novel. Penang is not what it was, golfwise.

On the other hand, Kuala Lumpur forges ahead from strength to strength, with magnificent new courses to ease congestion at Royal Selangor. During the Japanese occupation, an airstrip was built right across this splendid course and the remainder was used for army training and growing vegetables. But these were minor obstacles among those which have been overcome during the long dramatic history of the Royal Selangor Golf Club.

Nomadic golfers can say what they like (and they will) but for me Royal Selangor, flat as a pancake, has the stamp of greatness. The club has that indefinable something which is always noticed at the best golf centres in Great Britain, and having made that major declaration I hasten to add that the administration of Royal Selangor is now entirely in the hands of Malaysians. There are, of course, many British members who help with advice when asked, but this is a Malaysian show and so far as I could see it cannot be faulted.

Sprinkle a few deer on the course, and give cockney accents to the caddies, and instead of Royal Selangor golf you have Royal Windsor Park. There are two good-looking 18 hole courses, and one of 9 holes. The 'Old', where the championships are played, stretches to nearly 7,000 yards; the 'New' is shorter; and the 9 holes 'Suleiman' is preferred by ladies. They are skilfully laid out in parkland relieved with flowering trees, like 'flame of the forest', tembusus and acacias. The disposition of the bunkers (filled with exceptionally soft sand from a nearby tin mine) is particularly imaginative. All three courses are splendidly maintained under the directions of a young Indian, who was trained at the Selangor College of Agriculture; he asks for nothing more of life than the ability to give his members the best terrain for golf.

Two days before a Malaysian Championship, the Selangor course was struck by a typhoon which uprooted 110 trees. Can you imagine the chaos had this happened at Wentworth or Augusta National! The Malaysians were dismayed but not defeated. In short time the Office of Public Works and hundreds of willing helpers had cleared the mess and play began as scheduled.

That is what I liked about Royal Selangor. The club is a national affair of which everyone is tremendously proud. I don't suppose the hall porter at the Merlin Hotel (where we stayed) is a player, but when I mentioned golf at Royal Selangor, he immediately commented that it is 'the best in the world'. Maybe not. But one has the impression that the whole of the country, from the Tunku to the humblest caddie thinks so, and will do anything to keep it that way.

I had drinks and talk with Tun Sir Henry H.S. Lee, who was Malaysia's first Minister of Finance, and when we were there was the President of the Golf Association of Malaysia. Sir Henry has been a member of Royal Selangor since 1924, and played with the present Sultan's grandfather; he is the personification of gracious golf and does everything he can to preserve what is best in the game.

We touched on historical aspects of Royal Selangor and I learned that the club started in 1893—before the word Malaysia had been thought up—with 30 members, 5 holes, and a tent as clubhouse. Later a philanthropist gave 'a pavilion and a shed for horses'.

The talk with Sir Henry hoisted me on to my favourite hobby-horse—chasing facts about ancient golf. How about this? Immediately after the First World War, the Selangor club faced a major crisis. Play had always been on Petaling Hill, then, when the battle was over and folk were settling down to peaceful golf again, the government claimed the course as a public park. Local addicts were incensed but they found an answer.

Following an astonishing exchange of correspondence between the British Head of State and the President of the golf club—who happened to be the same person—agreement was reached whereby the club vacated the small course on Petaling Hill (where golf had been played around a Chinese cemetery) and took over 380 acres of forest reserve. This is the present course and any stretch of land less likely to be converted into a beautiful parkland golf course would be difficult to find. Part of the area was being used as a 'night-soil' disposal area; there were disused tin mines; and a swamp where sportsmen shot snipe. To make clearance more difficult, the nearby jungle was creeping in like a fast tide. It seemed a black outlook for the Selangor golfers, but they coped. The dismal area was tidied up and within a year it was a very fair golf course.

Committeemen at Royal Selangor are an ingenious breed. At one time the club owned a herd of cattle to keep the rough down and fertilise the fairways. Cash had always been scarce and there is nothing novel about this, but someone produced a new swimming pool and this simple addition doubled the membership in 1937. Now the membership is constant at 2,000 and bursting a little at the seams.

From the moment the Golf Widow and I passed through the Kuala Lampur airport barrier, Nobby Clarke and his charming missus took us in tow. They were the only contacts we had in Malaysia, a state of affairs that was quickly changed, for Nobby is an old-timer and introduced us to everyone we had to meet. He is past President, and past Captain of Royal Selangor and officiated during the difficult years of 1946/47/48. These worries, however, did not seem greatly to affect his golf for he was runner-up in the Malaysian Championship in 1949, winner of a Lucifer Trophy . . . and goodness knows what else.

With his friends Dick Chandler and Bill MacLeod, Nobby Clarke has probably done more to establish Malaysian golf than anyone.

To me his kindnesses were immense. What more could a chap do than relinquish his place in an established four-ball so that I could get a game immediately on arrival? That is what happened

Royal Selangor
KUALA LUMPUR

and off we went, Chandler, MacLeod, Jim Bottomley (Deputy British High Commissioner; the phoniest 19 handicap in Malaysia), and travel-tattered Houghton—with the Golf Widow and Nobby in attendance.

I hit some indifferent shots, but mostly, as was necessary on this trip, I asked questions. We got the story of how, faced with a considerable mess to clear after the Japanese occupation, Nobby decided to consult the General Commanding British Forces—who was a golfer.

'Look here, General,' said Nobby, 'if I could get some mechanical help it would make a tremendous difference to the speed of getting decent golf started.'

'Supposing I mount an exercise . . .' said the General.

Within days, bulldozers, scrapers, and a giant earth mover arrived at the club with a couple of dozen sappers and an N.C.O. who reported to Nobby for instructions. The big job was done beautifully.

Four years later, a senior officer who had arrived from the War Office to look into accounts, queried an item of 175,000 Malay dollars for an 'anti-malarial project'. Penetrating enquiries followed, and the golf club got the bill!

Undismayed, and remembering that attack is the best defence, Nobby saw the man from London and said: 'The club has always allowed military personnel to play golf at a greatly reduced rate. Now, if we were to send you a bill . . .'

A splendid compromise was reached and the man from the War Office effected an honourable withdrawal.

There are many stories of resourceful Britons in these far-flung outposts of golfdom, but the real interest now lies in the astonishing way the nationals are coping with the game. Malaysia has become a land of golf addicts, and it is pleasing to observe that the game progresses along the right lines. You won't find eight-player 'crocodiles' here. In fact, and this is strange, I had the impression in Kuala Lumpur that golf is more British in character than it is in Singapore—although the percentage of Britons participating must be less.

Mr Benny Lou is a senior Malaysian security officer. He is based in Kuala Lumpur and has been involved in all the crime and political problems you would expect. During the past fifteen years he has not often missed practising golf shots for two hours each day before breakfast. He starts at first light, bashes away, then hurries home for tea and eggs before going to his office at 9 a.m. Mr Lou says golf brings solace and allows him to forget the disagreeable things in life. I promised to look up Mr Lou's son who is a student at the Imperial College of Science in London University. Dad's handicap is 4.

Should he see these paragraphs, Mr Lou will no doubt be surprised. He may even be annoyed, although I hope not. We met on the putting green at the Royal Selangor Club, at about 6.30 a.m., an hour when you would hardly expect a queue on the first tee. But there was one, and I was part of it, along with Mr Yong, Secretary of the Club, Mr Lim, an athletic young badminton champion, and Mr Khoo, a most amusing fellow whom his friends call 'Mister Magoo'. He is in rubber.

We will come back to that four-ball, mentioned along with Benny Lou, merely to highlight Royal Selangor at dawn and the type of people who have taken to golf seriously enough to sacrifice beauty sleep.

As in Singapore, early morning is golftime in Kuala Lumpur, and this applies all over Malaysia. It is normal for the mad British, or even Americans, to turn out in the dark for golf, but somehow or other one did not expect to find serious Malaysian businessmen on the first tee at 6 a.m. It came as an even greater surprise to learn that Tunku Abdul Rahman, Malaysia's Prime Minister, and at least six of his ministers also play early morning golf.

I don't suppose that for the rest of my life I will ever again have a chance to play golf with a Prime Minister. I mentioned what happened in Singapore, and here in Kuala Lumpur my game with the Tunku suffered a similar fate. Our golf date was cancelled because of an emergency cabinet meeting and when the Secretary announced the sad news he said 'The Tunku says he is more sorry than you are.'

In the previously mentioned four-ball with my new Malaysian friends, we followed the Minister of Lands and Mines, the Thailand Ambassador (a leftie), the Thai Military Attaché, and a good player who I think was the Sultan of Selangor. Later, we met the Sultan and his brother for drinks in the clubhouse and I heard the story of the Sultan's famous hole-in-one at the 15th. He was playing with the King of Malaysia and the incident so thrilled him that the match was abandoned and they hurried back to the clubhouse, and 'phoned the Sultan's friends to attend an immediate celebration party. The Sultan now has a private golf course in the grounds of his new palace built on the top of a hill at Klang, about twenty miles from K.L. Naturally enough, the 'ace' ball is mounted in a place of honour.

Malaysia consists of eleven states, nine of which are ruled by hereditary Sultans. Malacca and Penang have 'Governors'. The powers of these 'rulers' are limited to local issues, but among themselves they elect the king for the entire federation and he reigns for a term of five years.

The present Agong (King) of Malaysia plays golf at the Royal Selangor Club about three times a week. The Tunku seldom misses a few daily holes and to make things easier, Data Bill MacLeod made the Prime Minister a present of a white electric buggy, the only one in Kuala Lumpur. On the course, little bridges have been built over the water hazards to take the buggy which, for safety, is kept in the Secretary's garden.

Possibly the best player among Asia's golfing politicians and diplomats is Tun Razak, Deputy Prime Minister of Malaysia; but there is little doubt who was the keenest. This laurel goes to

Golf plays a major role in Malaysian diplomacy!

the Agong, who had been Sultan of Perlis. Of him there are many good stories.

In golfing communities all over the world, a ball is the accepted unit for wagers. In Malaya, these are always paid in the form of signed chits which are negotiable at the pro's shop, or can be used as payment when you lose a game. Sometimes the bets elevate a bit and it is not unusual to receive (or pay out) chits amounting to six, ten or a dozen balls. Periodically, the club calls in all chits and they have to be presented at the professional's shop for merchandise. The story is told that the golf addicted King once went to Mike Kelly, the professional, with enough ball chits not only to get a complete new set of clubs for himself but also a set, with a trolley, for the Queen!

CHAPTER SEVENTEEN

Shorty, Tom, and the Cameron Highlands

OF THE MANY kinky addicts we met on this tour I can think of no one who had a better tale to tell than 'Shorty' Laws. One of his golfing adventures took place at Ipoh, capital of the tin territory.

Motor north from Kuala Lumpur for about a hundred miles and you enter the best golf country in Malaysia. This is the Kuita Valley, probably the largest alluvial tin deposit in the world; right in the middle stands Ipoh, once a flourishing town but now a little slowed down. That doesn't apply to the golf club, which promotes the Northern Malaysian Championship each January during the holiday for Chinese New Year.

Before we describe Shorty's big moment at Ipoh, you will better appreciate the type of things that happen to this colourful chap when you consider his record in a local tournament. Some golfers drift happily along, unnoticed in the quiet backwaters of the game. Others are constantly the centre of fireworks. Shorty is among the latter. In the quarter-finals of this competition, playing from a handicap of 6, he met a man whose handicap was 13; the latter conceded the match when Shorty was 8 up after 9 holes. In the semi-final, Shorty's opponent had a handicap of 22. The same thing happened and when Shorty was 8 up after 9 holes, his adversary conceded. Then came the final. Shorty met a 2 handicap tiger who, after 9 holes, was 8 up—so Shorty conceded!

Yorkshire produced John Dennis Laws. He is out in Malaysia selling industrial equipment and his life seems to have been a succession of freak happenings, mostly disagreeable to Shorty, but usually amusing for his pals.

When a player in the Ipoh Championship disturbed a nest of bees at hole 4 it was inevitable that they should swarm on Shorty

Laws while he was putting on green 18. He had been told to lie flat on his face and keep still if ever menaced this way. Shorty did just that, but still they attacked.

In extreme pain he fled into the clubhouse with the bees buzzing around his head, arms and bare knees. Not until he had retreated to the locker room and submerged in a full bath did the disappointed bees buzz from the clubhouse. Members who had taken refuge in closed cars eventually began to emerge. They found Shorty in a bad way. There was no doctor present but luckily the club Captain was a vet and perhaps the patient benefited from the anti-histamine horse-pill which was given to him, crushed up in beer.

What occurred afterwards could only happen to Shorty Laws. In the locker room, a dozen golfers gathered around their naked friend and quickly organised a sweepstake to guess the number of stings! With eyebrow pluckers borrowed from the ladies section, each barb was carefully removed and counted. There were 148 and the kitty went to 150 because that was nearest. The winner bought Shorty a series of well-earned stingahs to round off the happy day.

When a writer finds a Shorty Laws he has to be squeezed dry. On board ship during a poker game, Shorty once swallowed a florin which had been slipped into his beer. While he spluttered, one of his friends thumped his back, and another planked down a pound note calling heads or tails for when the florin was coughed up!

Many brave Britons have elected to make their homes on the equator and it surprises me how excellently they adapt themselves to conditions and climate so different from home. In this respect, Tom Verity, from Keighley in Yorkshire, is outstanding.

Tom has been in Malaysia for years. He was professional at Royal Selangor, fought against the guerillas, worked as a tea planter in the mountains, and when we visited him Tom was carving out a tremendous golf course from rubber plantations located in the south of Selangor.

Sungei Way, by the Petaling tin mine, was chosen as the site for a great new 7,000 yards championship golf course. There will also be an adjoining 9 holes course which will be government subsidised to put golf within reach of everyone's pocket.

Tom was standing in the doorway of a large wooden house on

a hill in a rubber forest. Once, the plantation manager had lived there with his servants. Now it was empty, excepting for a table, a beer ´fridge, a bed, and bats clinging to the ceiling. But it was Tom Verity's home and from here he directed the herculean task of fashioning fairways from trees and jungle; levelling off, draining and building greens; moving earth so that grass could grow where the metal ore comes to the surface, and so on . . . For the job, Tom has bulldozers, earth scrapers, tractors, and about a hundred coolies.

We bumped along in Verity's jeep and wondered how it was possible to fashion a golf course in such territory. Yet, the work progressed and already the layout was taking shape. There were fine swinging fairways, platform tees and kidney-shaped greens. Even some grass planting had been started and on smoothed fairways, at yard intervals, sprigs of spreading grass had been pressed in. Tom assured us that this grows 'as soon as you turn your head'.

Everything develops at an alarming pace in Malaysia and if left the undergrowth of the edging jungle could steal back the clearings in a matter of weeks. One must keep up the constant task of hacking back the growth. When tropical rains come, work has to stop, and it sometimes takes days to release the bulldozers from the clinging mud and chop off the strangling tendons of the trees.

The design for Sungei Way is the work of a famous Japanese architect named Seiichi Inouye, who was specially commissioned by the Tunku to make the best golf course in Asia, disregarding expense.

Sungei Way could become that and if it does let's hope that Tom Verity will be remembered. I couldn't help thinking that the Yorkshire lad was a long way from Keighley, but I'd wager he never returns.

Grasshopping from one golf club to another can be great fun, especially in out of the way places. Kluang is south of Sungei Way, in the state of Johore on the main road. For years there had been 'a bit of a course' there, but some men of the Tom Verity kidney got cracking in the late 'fifties and with the help of Nobby Clarke, then President of the Malaysian Golf Association, the Kluang course was granted an official standard scratch score. Air Force personnel, stationed near, removed boulders, filled in holes, and the game blossomed. The surface is just cow grass, and where the fairways can be cut especially short that is a green.

But Kluang has golf, and now the members bravely play inter-club matches.

Soldiers, sailors and airmen of all nationalities have done much for golf and it gladdened me to learn that when the British handed back the old Kuala Lumpur airfield, the first thing the Royal Malaysian Air Force did was to use most of the land for a golf course. A senior officer said: 'I'd sooner have my men out playing golf than at home making children.'

There is another Services course at Port Dickson, in the State of Negri Sembilan, where young men from the Royal Malaysian Military College (with some chaps from Sandhurst) have 'polished up' a bit of land behind the college. On this delightful site near the sea the game flourishes.

That is the sort of thing we found all over Malaysia. Even at Kota Bharu and Kuantan, on the remote and unspoilt east coast, there are keen golfers and some of them I am glad to say are Europeans.

The 'happy hacker' spirit is perfectly illustrated at Seremban. This course, before the war, formed part of a race-track and was plotted on land which subsequently was required for mining. Undismayed, the members got to work with a tin dredge and actually moved the surface land of the course to a hilly area nearby. As one would expect, with this type of dauntless human material Seremban club takes on anybody in golfing combat. Then, afterwards, they produce the most wonderful curry meals with plenty of iced beer to cool down the tonsils.

Malaysian railways stretch in two long arms, one going to Kota Bharu on the east coast, the other to the small state of Perlis in the extreme north-west. The tracks join south of Kuala Lumpur and run down to Singapore. The Sentul Sports Club was formed for the benefit of the conscientious railway employees. As to be expected, there is a golf section with a waiting list as long as your arm.

When we were there most golf clubs in Malaysia were over-crowded. At Taiping there is a hole where you can slice a shot into the gaol. On one Sunday morning, a player who had to collect his ball said: 'Anyway, it will get me out of this crowd!' Taiping has the heaviest rainfall in Malaysia, which is why the park course and gardens are green and beautifully flowered. There are always compensations.

My mention of Penang did not do justice to the keen band of golfers who are 'managing' with a 9 holes course. Formerly, the club had a famous (though hilly) 18 holes course over which some great personalities performed. Then, like many other golf clubs during the war, Penang rather disintegrated. The course at the time of writing is in and around the race-track and the golf is run in conjunction with the Turf Club. Unlike Bangkok (also on a racecourse) there is no play on race days at Penang. I am doubtful whether the priorities are correct, but I am in no doubt whatever that I shall be bombarded with criticism letters from the hard core of Penang golfers who deserve better.

Nearly 5,000 feet up in the mountains that run like a spine dividing eastern and western Malaysia, there is the holiday resort of Fraser's Hill. The 9 holes course is on the top of a mountain and has the reputation 'rather hazardous golf'. We didn't play there, but I have the impression that on a busy day golf balls fly in all directions. The course is on a plateau among the hills and some fairways cross in a confined area that is reminiscent of certain Scottish courses.

Malaysian businessmen, cooling off in a mountain guest house, often learn their golf at Fraser's Hill; they should choose a roomier spot.

But for good golf at a delightfully cool altitude, players in these parts go to Cameron Highlands, not far from Ipoh, and about a hundred interesting motoring miles north of K.L.

You take the main highway to Tapah, then branch off to the right up a winding mountain road, and when you reach Cameron Highlands you are not only in a resort with a Scottish name, but also you will see other signs of Scotland. This is a hill station with a first-class hotel on the edge of the golf course, good smaller ones, and some nearby inexpensive guest houses. Up in the mountains there is a large hydro-electric scheme and it is the intention to keep a stretch of water well stocked with the right sort of fish for good sport.

Malaysians are lucky to have this splendid resort. The golf course is a hilly 9 holes with trees, good greens and a winding burn. Extra pines have been planted on the course, but most of the trees were there before the undergrowth jungle was cleared.

Life is full of discord and I must now toss a jarring note into this harmonious scene. From three sound sources I was told that

Henry Cotton had something nice to say about hole 7. In fact, I was told that the maestro had openly declared this to be one of the best golf holes he had ever played. There is a daunting drive with a carry over a stream, which has to be very straight to pass beyond the stream over a hill with trees on one side and deep jungle on the other. The ball then drops some thirty or forty feet on to a lower level fairway and the second shot involves a carry over another bigger stream which crosses the fairway diagonally some fifty yards short of the green. A four on the seventh hole at the Cameron Highlands is one of the most satisfying birdies one can make.

On return to England I mentioned to Henry that they still remember what he said about hole 7 on his visit to the mountains of Malaysia.

'Strange,' said Henry. 'I've never even been to the country!' Which just shows.

Malaysian golfers have fun. One Christmas, at Cameron Highlands, the King's team played the Tunku's team and the affair lasted for four days. Wives came along for the feastings given by the King, the Sultan of Selangor, and finally by the Tunku, who sent to Ipoh for a troupe of Rongeng (Malaysian) dancers and a special band.

On these joyous occasions, who cares if the golf competition rules are bent a little. When the Tunku was invited to take a team to play the Sultan of Kedah's side, the latter, believing that his men would lose rather badly at normal match play, ruled that the contest should be decided by the net aggregate scores in four-ball matches. Holing everything out, games took about three hours for nine holes! But no-one minded. Lunch came after nine holes, then the matches were completed in the afternoon.

Tunku Abdul Rahman once received a present from Thailand's Deputy Defence Minister, Air Chief Marshal Dawee Chulasappya. It was a putter equipped with a battery, bell, horn, searchlight, and tape measure. Along with the gift, there was a note: 'When your opponent is about to putt, honk the horn and clang the bell. The tape measure is calculated to give your adversary an inferiority complex. The searchlight will enable you to play all night. If you still cannot win with this device, give up golf and take up fishing'.

Malaysians have two endearing qualities; they are warmly hos-

The 8th on the 'Old' KUALA LUMPUR

The 8th hole, Royal Selangor

pitable and have a great sense of humour. In a four-ball with Malaysian friends, I had a caddie who kept the other carriers roaring with laughter. The talk was Malay so of course I could not understand, but my partner explained that the boy was giving a running commentary of our play in verse to the other caddies. Try hitting a golf ball under those circumstances!

Caddies are used nearly always in the seven countries we visited on the tour. There is no shortage of this kind of labour and payment is low. Most clubs look after their caddies and see they are properly trained. At Royal Selangor, for example, the 400 registered boys are classified as 1st class (blue shirts) and 2nd class (purple shirts), after tests by a representative of the greens committee. The boys have 'leaders' and an organisation for training and discipline. Their pay is two-and-a-half Malaysian dollars (about 6s.) for 18 holes, with a permissible half-dollar tip.

Most of the Malaysian caddies work hard and, like their patrons, love to gamble on the game. In fact, they gamble on anything. There is a kind of woodpecker bird called the *tok-tok*; caddies put ten cents each in the kitty, then guess the number of toks!

So many heads of Malaysian states have become keen golfers that I hesitate to single one out. However, Tun Malik (*tun* means 'Lord'), the Governor of Malacca, must be mentioned.

His Excellency, a keen 12 handicap golfer, was the prime mover behind the splendid course in the state capital which Cyril Horne of Singapore helped to lay out. There used to be a flat, short course down by the shore, with the clubhouse in the middle and protected by wire netting because you actually had to play over it! But now Malacca has the magnificent new course. This, and Tom Verity's Sungei Way, could well develop into the best in South-East Asia.

Malacca was once the most important trading post in the east. A Portuguese chronicler in the 15th century wrote: 'Whoever is lord in Malacca has his hands on the throat of Venice'. That may have been so four hundred years ago, but to-day the lord of Malacca has his hands on a golf club, and this applies to all Malaysia's leaders.

The name of the capital should be Kuala LumPAR!

CHAPTER EIGHTEEN

Round-up

OVER-GOLFED AND SLIGHTLY TRAVEL-WEARY, but stimulated and instructed beyond all measure, we reached the end of
the tour.

A final four-ball with new Malay friends. Dinner at the 'Spotted
Dog' with Nobby Clarke, Dick Chandler (high priests of golf in
Malaysia) and their ladies. Then bed, and the usual dawn rush to
the airport.

'We are passing over the tip of Sumatra at 36,000 feet; our
speed is 600 miles an hour', said the B.O.A.C. Skipper of our
V.C.10.

The home green was rapidly approaching, so here, for your
consideration, I submit my scorecard.

Of the thirty-three golf courses which we inspected, Hirono,
in Japan, is the one that most deserves the hackneyed tag 'the
finest test of golf'. At the Japan Golf Association, the Director
said (possibly risking his life!) that Hirono is Japan's best. I
would go further and declare this golf course to be the best in
the Far East and, from a design point of view, comparable with
any in the world.

For scenic beauty I choose the Valley course, in the Philippines,
and I am only hoping that, when the proprietary shareholders
build on their plots of land, the lovely hills will not be spoilt.

The Valley Golf and Country Club has also the most imaginative, well-appointed clubhouse we visited, and I am quite
certain there is not another even remotely like it.

You can toss up between Royal Selangor and the Island Club,
Singapore, for the best greens in the Far East. Both use Seragoon
grass, which is native to Singapore and flourishes in moist heat.
These surfaces are better than most in Britain.

For cheery surroundings, with a 'guzz in the dorm' atmosphere,
I choose Fanling, Royal Hong Kong. Things are right and kindly

here. A club competition was scheduled for the day the M.C.C. cricketers stopped off; nevertheless, free times were left on the crowded starting sheet 'just in case' some of the visitors wanted to play.

Fanling also takes the prize for the best (and cheapest) club meals and dormy-house accommodation.

For the ultimate in first-class swanky golf I declare a tie between Wack Wack, Manila, and Kawana, Japan, where the adjoining 'Gleneagles type' hotel (fortunately for my pocket) is out of this world.

As an unusual but thrilling golfing experience, I choose Royal Bangkok—in the heart of Thailand's capital (smiling girls, with neat waists)—where you see an exhibition of incredible underwater swimming by your 'klong caddie' every time you slice into a canal.

The girls in Japan were by far the best caddies I had on the tour. Not only do they know golf thoroughly, but also they sweetly sympathise in a language you don't have to understand every time you make a bad shot.

Most colourful and certainly most energetic spreader of the golf gospel whom we met was Cyril Horne, pocket professional at Bukit, Singapore. His teaching patter is fun, and the 'special for prime ministers' brand of instruction is worth at least four votes for Great Britain at the United Nations.

Finally, laurels for the Bombay Presidency Golf Club at Chembur, where addicts cheerfully endure prohibition, equally dry fairways, and over-used golf balls (because they can't be imported), yet extend a wonderfully warm welcome to visitors.

So there you have it. Golf in the Far East is a fabulous, red-hot (especially on the 100° days!) adventure. Only rarely did we find courses comparable with Britain's best, but by gosh, give me Asia for addicts! Never have I seen such dedication. Golf is increasingly popular in Britain and America, but our enthusiasm is luke-warm compared to what is happening in the East.

For a start, take Japan, where hundreds of new hackers hatch out daily on driving ranges and improvised pitches on the roofs of nearly every factory and office block. The manufacture of golf equipment is becoming a major industry; instead of buying motor cars, addicts are saving to pay golf club entry fees that are soaring as land prices increase. Golf has been nationally popular for only a decade, but already in Japan there are four times the number of players that we have in Great Britain—where we have seriously golfed for more than a hundred years! An official told me that at least a dozen Japanese professionals will be ready to wrestle for the British and American Open Championships in 1968!